Journey to Claim

My Buried Soul

An Alchemical Life

By

Camilla Leon

Also by the author

Tales of Magic and Transformation:
Book One: The Dragon and the Toad
Book: Two: Haven Island

First published in 2022 by Cassiel Books
2nd Edition published 2024
3rd Edition: Updated and Extended, published 2025
ISBN: 978-1-912484-93-5
© Diana Hadlow (aka Camilla Leon) 2022
Photographs and original artworks © Diana Hadlow
Chameleon illustration © Andrew Plant

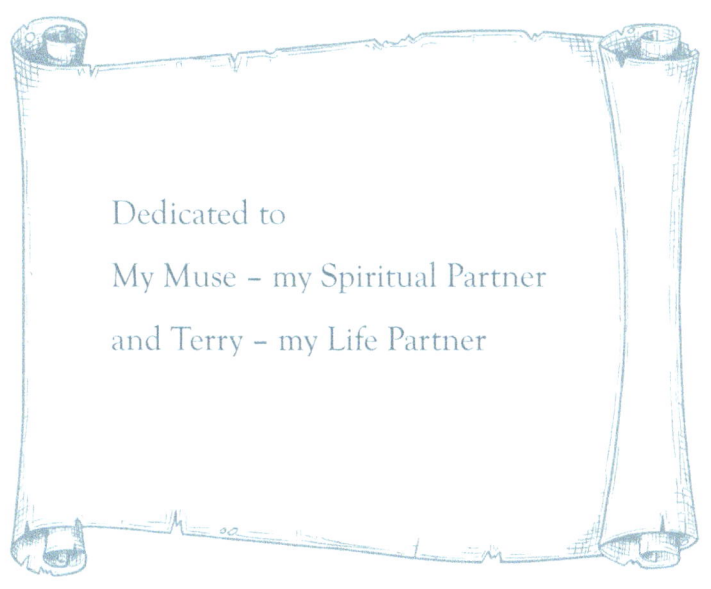

Dedicated to

My Muse – my Spiritual Partner

and Terry – my Life Partner

Acknowledgements:

With special thanks to
Julie Webster for her friendship and remarkable IT support.
John Woodman for his steadfast encouragement and friendship.
Bob Morley for his friendship and poetic inspiration.
And Brendan Taylor, whose courage, dedication and commitment to
his drive for wholeness is inspirational.
Much gratitude to Angie Anderson for assistance
with the publishing of this book.

The Song of My Soul

Life, the Consciousness

That floods through me,

A gift – Enormous

Magnificent and Radiant.

I did nothing to earn this,

A gift pure and simple

That only requires me to live it,

Allow it expression,

Revel in the joy of being.

21.06.21

SUMMARY OF CONTENTS

NOTE TO THE READER

This book is primarily about the spiritual journey and I have therefore chosen to separate the content into two parts.

PART ONE: focuses on everything relating to the spiritual journey and provides whatever information is necessary to put the reader into the state of mind of the author at the particular part of the journey being covered and guidance on how to approach the poems.

PART TWO: provides a rational underpinning of the journey as recorded in Part One. It describes 'Why and How' the book was written. In addition, using academic sources where necessary it outlines: how the poems came into being; the main theoretical models used and how they are employed to organise the poems; how the poems are selected; why there are three cycles and the reasons why these and the gaps between them vary so much in time. Also included are any other academic, theoretical and psychological issues which were triggered during the writing of this book.

PART ONE CONTENTS
The Spiritual Journey

PART TWO CONTENTS
Supporting Material

HOW TO READ THIS BOOK

This is a book about feelings and emotions. My soul was reaching out to me through the poems in order to heal the split in my psyche.

I had learned to think – not feel…

I had learned to 'fit in' to what was expected of me…

and neither route would lead to happiness or fulfilment. So, my Muse / Spiritual Guide stepped in to help.

To facilitate getting into the story I recommend the following:

1. **Read the Preface.** This establishes the relationship between my Muse / Spiritual Guide and me as we set out on the journey.

2. **Read the Introduction in full.** Here I introduce myself and the circumstances of my early life which provided the motivation and jumping off point for the rest of the book.

It presents the goal of the journey and how it is to be attained.

It provides a Synopsis of the narrative.

It also provides guidance on how the poems are presented.

3. **Read the Preludes** as you approach each new Cycle of Poems, for this provides you with sufficient information for you to be able to relate to my state of mind as I set out on the next bit of the journey.

4. Then start on the poems.

PREFACE

I was born curious, a natural seeker. What made me curious was that I was convinced that there were two worlds – two rivers to explore, which flowed side by side and the one I was most curious about, was the underground river that fed the surface one. I didn't tell anyone, for I felt this underground river was in forbidden territory. It was my secret and one I protected, kept hidden close to my heart.

I was seven years old when I got confirmation that this forbidden realm was inhabited. I know I was seven because I realised it was unusual for a little girl of my age to be contacted by someone from the forbidden land.

The voice told me that I was dearly loved by my Daddy, if not by my mother, who did her best to care for me, but couldn't love me. This being had taken a big risk by challenging the rule that prohibited the crossing of the boundaries between the two worlds, for she was concerned because of the desperate unhappiness I felt. Only the force of her argument against this rule earned her the permission she needed.

It was her love and the proof she had given me of the other world's reality that fed my determination to seek out this other realm and which supported me as I grew up.

It was fourteen years later before I heard from her again. She made her presence known by giving me poems which was the way she usually communicated with me. At first these were joyous poems that I allowed into my mind, reassuring me again of the love that created them, for I knew they came from my muse from the forbidden land.

She became my guide, prompting my actions, so that I would take side tributaries that led through the borderlands of our two worlds. I trusted her implicitly, so that when the path led through territories that were dangerous and scary, I knew my muse was holding my hand and giving me courage to follow where she led.

'Does everyone have a second Mother like you?' I asked.

She smiled and replied "Yes of course sweetheart, how else could anyone know the way, although I am often known as a spiritual guide. The problem is not everyone is curious. Some prefer to struggle in the world they know, satisfied with the distractions and animal comforts they can buy. They fall asleep and are deluded into believing their dreams and illusions of happiness are real.

Sometimes it is necessary to give them a shock, to wake them up to the pitiful state of their world because they have neglected their responsibility for caring for it. And for others it is only when they get lost and are desperate for help that they are needy enough to pay attention to my voice."

So began the journey to this other land, where the river that keeps feeding this world has its source.

My muse, as I came to call her, warned me it could be hard to confront the guardians of the borderlands, who were there to protect the unwary travellers from entering into forbidden territory. Only those accompanied by her could vanquish the monsters and demons on the way, for they were inadequate to break the spell of protection and courage she afforded me.

'Where do the monsters and demons come from?' I asked her.

"You create them yourself, not intentionally, but as a result of the fears you have developed because of the mistaken beliefs you have been taught. Each time you vanquish them you grow closer to the truth.

Trust me, regardless of the perils, for I will never let you down or abandon you, but it is you who will have to summon all your courage and commitment to keep following the path I show you. Keep faith in me, for I love you and will not leave you unsupported."

'Why are there two worlds?' I asked her.

"So you can grow strong enough to cross the borderlands. Every time you meet an obstacle or demon that scares you, you have to grow another bit of yourself, until you are strong enough to meet your other half, who lives in my world."

'My other half!' I gasped, 'What do you mean?'

"Well, the other half of you lives in my world and is waiting for you to join her. Only by growing your willingness to continue to battle through the fierce undergrowth and challenges of the hinterland that borders your world, can you make your way towards her, where she is waiting."

'How will I know her?' I asked, puzzled that I hadn't even known she existed.

My muse laughed, "Oh, you will meet her first as an enemy, for you will see her as a threat to yourself. Only as you become willing to recognise that she has a power that augments your own will the two of your come to an arrangement that will suit you both. For you also have something to offer her, the gift of consciousness.

Come now my sweet child, let us begin the adventure. It may take some time, but you have plenty of that."

This is the real story of my life – the tale of how I listened and was guided by my muse. I appeared to live in the surface world, but the important reality concerning my forays through the borderland were recorded and conveyed to me by the poems she fed me.

INTRODUCTION

Welcome to you, my reader. My hope is that you will find in the following record of my spiritual journey, inspiration to pursue your own spiritual path, and thus discover for yourself the truth about who you are and be blessed with the support of your spiritual guides.

There is a book on my shelf entitled '*This Tree grows out of Hell*', a title which seems to describe the beginning of the spiritual journey for so many people. It is precisely when one feels broken and in despair that the motivation to change one's life comes into focus and may provide you with the desire to seek your own true destiny.

Dante Aligheri's quote from the *Divine Comedy* is more optimistic stating: '*The Path to Paradise begins in Hell*'.

Another quote I came across recently is so appropriate that I felt I also had to include it here:

'Art and music must come from the heart.....Even the darkest places need to be brought into the light of day, or else they will grow until they swallow a man whole.'
(Harkness, D. ("The Book of Life" 2014 p.301).

———————

Let me introduce myself. My name is Diana. (Camilla Leon is my pen-name). I was born just after the Second World War. I assume my conception was a celebration of its ending, yet my arrival was a disappointment to my mother. She had always wanted four sons and my difficult birth put an end to her wishes. As the third child and one who ended her child-bearing years, she had to content herself with two sons and a daughter.

This is not an autobiography in the normal sense, but a record of my inner journey, for I am a mystic by temperament and struggled to find my direction, saddled as I was with the disadvantage of being a girl, with the local Methodist church my only spiritual resource.

I was seven years old when I first heard my inner voice come to my rescue. I had just been confronted with the naked hostility my mother felt for me, a legacy from her own childhood. My inner wise woman came to my rescue in response to the extreme distress I felt. She reminded me that even if my mother didn't love me, my Daddy certainly did.

This voice from my unconscious had breached the wall between my conscious ego and the unconscious part of me, out of the pressing need of the child in me, and provided me with a sense of being supported by this source of inner strength.

It was fourteen years before I heard this inner voice again. I came to call her my muse for she communicated with me via poetry. Through poetry I learnt to give a voice to the part of myself I had to bury – the rejected part. It was the fact I was female that had earned my mother's rejection of me.

I learned to survive by denying a huge part of myself – my feminine soul. Ostensibly I was a good obedient child. I learned to keep my mouth shut, to keep my own counsel and study hard as my ticket to freedom.

Thus, I earned my freedom, but at the cost of denying my sense of myself. It took me years of trial and error to begin to know myself;

many years of counselling and therapy to learn to love myself and the part of me I called my 'Inner Child' that I had been forced to 'bury alive' in order to survive.

But that was not the end of it. How could I make amends to the part of me that I had buried alive and abandoned. I had to learn to forgive myself for doing what my mother had done, rejecting the feminine part of myself and that took time.

I was well into my seventies when I thought of writing this book but I wasn't sure what purpose it might serve, so I asked my muse (my spiritual guide). She replied that it provided a record of the physical, emotional, psychological and spiritual experiences that I had lived through during the stages of my spiritual journey.

As it was written by a woman, it could serve as a bridge between the various metaphysical and theoretical models of this, which were often described by men in elitist jargon which was difficult to understand. The poems themselves might also offer support, comfort and some validation of their experiences to other pilgrims on a similar journey.

Writing poems is, for me, like communing with a trusted and intimate confidante. The need to express something is often experienced as a tension in my body, a sense that 'something needs to be born' and I have to get myself somewhere safe so I can 'give birth'.

It is important to add that I had no idea what the poem would be about until I read it on the page. Sometimes it felt like I was taking dictation, at other times that I was being dripped a gestalt of meaning in bits that I had to translate into words.

In retrospect, it is obvious why I did not know the content of the poems, for the poems themselves were the means by which my abandoned soul was trying to get my attention. The buried Goddess – my abandoned soul – was reaching out to me through these poems so that I could begin to reclaim her.

Writing poems has always been an intensely personal and secret activity which I regarded as sacred, belonging to my inner spiritual life, although I did not at the time recognise their full significance as the voice of my soul.

Each of these poems is like a snapshot of a particular moment in time. Their value is in their truthfulness, for they were not intended for anyone but me, to reveal to me my unconscious emotions and feelings and what I needed to do to heal myself. I regard them as gifts from my muse.

Some of these may be difficult to read because the emotions expressed are ugly, shameful or painful, but therein resides their honesty. However, these are balanced with later poems of joy and relief, expressed as I move out of hell and towards freedom.

It is true that writing poems inspired by my muse gave me a growing sense of self-awareness and some direction, but my life was energised by a spiritual hunger – a divine homesickness – which kept me seeking for a way home, my true spiritual home. The mystic poet Rainer Maria Rilke expresses this beautifully: *"You (God) the great homesickness we could never shake off."*

I explored many religions and spiritual pathways. One of these, alchemy, provided a paradigm that I could relate to. I had written hundreds of poems recording my journey, and I wondered whether the stages described in the alchemical process might provide a helpful conceptual framework for the journey I had already undertaken. It provided a broad understanding of the spiritual purpose of our incarnation into this world, a realm of opposites in which each of us has to search for and integrate the unconscious half of ourselves.

We look for our soul-mate out there in the world, and may find someone who is able to reflect back to us the unconscious half of ourselves, so that we can learn to embrace it. No wonder opposites attract. However, the opposites we need to unite in order to become spiritually whole are those within us.

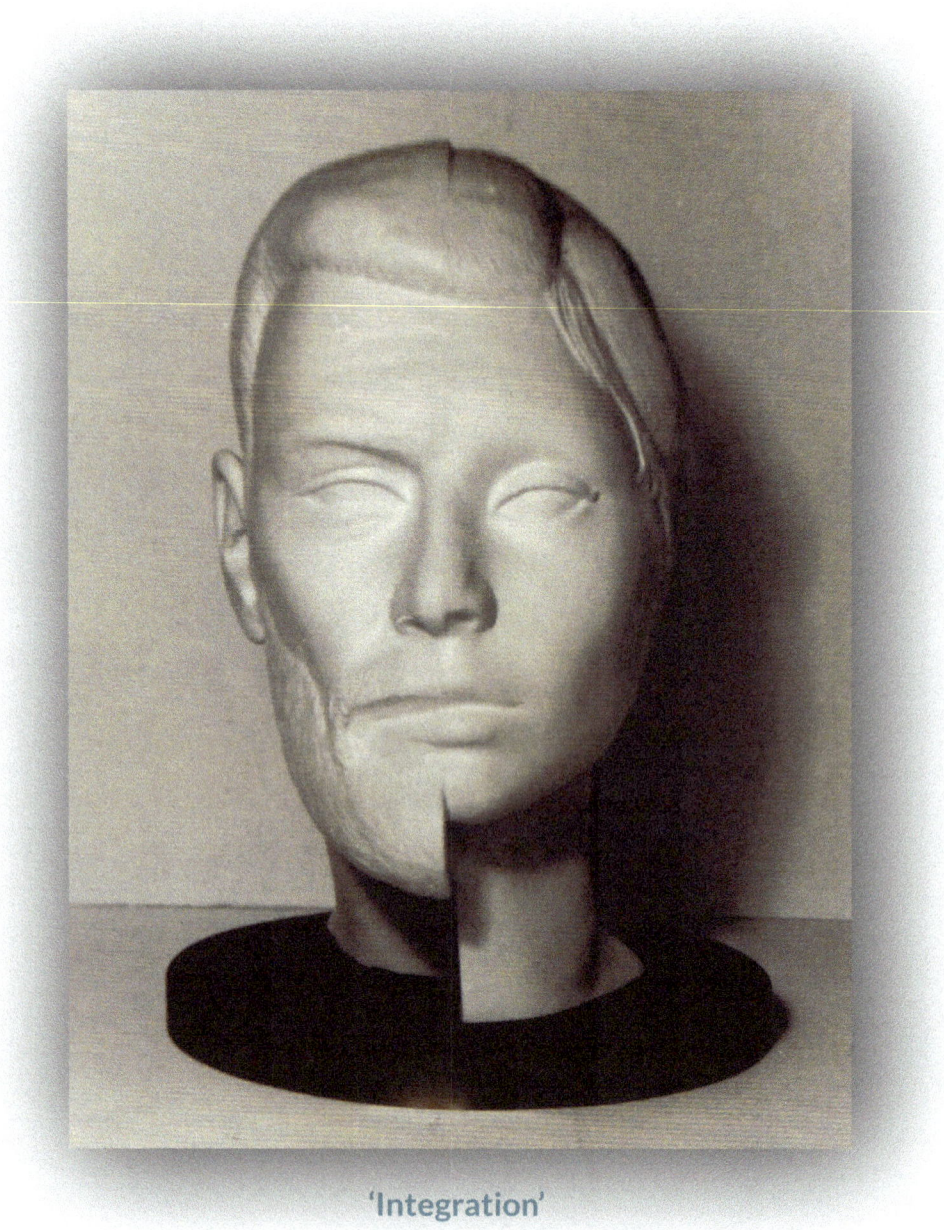

'Integration'

THE TRUE SELF

The True Self is the term used for the goal of the journey I am considering in this book. Other terms used for it are the Psyche or the Soul, but I will use the Self, which is not to be confused with the little personal self.

The **Self** is the ordering and unifying centre of the **Total Psyche** – the Conscious and the Unconscious, just as the **Ego** is the centre of the **Personality**. In other words, the Ego is the seat of SUBJECTIVE identity, while the Self is the seat of OBJECTIVE identity.

We are born into the Self, and the Ego develops from it. In very general terms the development of the Ego occupies the first half of life and it is this which provides the individual with CONSCIOUSNESS.

Only once a strong Ego is formed can the Self assume greater active influence over the individual. If there is no strong Ego, the Self would overwhelm it, as it has much more power. It is for this reason that the presence of the Self becomes more noticeable during the second half of life.

The Self is the SOURCE OF LIFE – the Fountain of our Being, and experientially it is regarded as the SUPREME PSYCHIC AUTHORITY, our personal deity.

The connection between the Self and the Ego is vitally important to psychic health. It gives foundation, structure and security to the Ego and also provides energy, interest, meaning and purpose. When the connection is broken the result is emptiness, despair, meaninglessness, and in extreme cases, psychosis or suicide.

This connection is termed the Ego/Self axis and it is initiated through the relationship between the child and its parents, as its Ego begins to develop out of its unconsciousness. The child's connection with the Self is largely identical with his relationship with his parents. Hence if the relationships are faulty, the child's contact with his inner centre of being will likewise be faulty.

For further information on the above, I refer you to 'Ego and Archetype' by Edward F. Edinger, which is included in Appendix C. Bibliography.

How to Create the Self

The way to create the Self is to unite the conscious with the unconscious mind. This is facilitated by the Transcendent Function in the psyche which bridges the two opposites. (*For information on the Transcendent Function, see Ch. 13.*) Although I did not realise it, I was generating the Self throughout my life as I received the poems from the unconscious and then wrote them down consciously, thus uniting the opposites.

––––––––––––––

Synopsis : A summary of the narrative

Sharing my spiritual journey through poems is an authentic way to share the journey with you but it is piecemeal and not a smooth narrative. So, I feel providing you with a summary of the whole journey will enable you to accommodate the inevitable 'jumps' in the narrative provided by the poems.

The voice that expresses itself in the poems *is* the voice of my abandoned soul. She cries out for recognition "a child's voice crying in the wilderness". The record of my spiritual journey is that of her healing and emancipation as my ego comes to recognise, accept, and love her as the fundamental expression of the soul that previously she had not known existed.

The shadow side of the soul, the buried Goddess, contains all that was rejected by the ego – the conscious mind – and expresses her anguish at having been unacknowledged and having to bear the burden of all the rejected feelings that the ego had refused to acknowledge. The ego has to come to terms with the fact she had abandoned this child of her soul in order to survive in our ego driven culture. Thus, the voice of the ego also appears in some of the poems.

The confrontation between the Goddess – the unconscious soul – and the ego is a shocking one for the ego. A powerful numinous experience that threatens to overwhelm her, but the Goddess is not there to scare the ego, but to invite her to accept the power and love she has to offer.

There is a power struggle between them initially as the ego wants to stay in control and the buried Goddess is intent on establishing her rightful place and power within the relationship. Occasional, breaks in their contact clarify to the ego exactly what it is the Goddess brings to their bond, for without her the ego feels depersonalised. The Goddess – our soul – is what gives us our personal element.

As they become familiar with each other and recognise that they can augment their power by co-operating together, they form a strong alliance and become a Whole Human Being. This does not mean the human being is perfect, but it does mean the person is whole. It is only once this stage has been reached that the individual is ready to be initiated into spiritual awakening, which follows in the latter part of the book. However, spiritual awakening is a process and lasts a lifetime.

Name Changes

In order to follow the narrative, you need to be aware of the name changes that occur as I begin to 'own' the characters in the story as being parts of myself, and consequently the relationships between them modify.

Initially, Ego and I are the narrators.

The Soul is identified variously as Psyche, Muse, Spiritual Guide, Inner Wise Woman, Goddess, Self, Guardian of the Threshold and the Shadow, depending on the context.

Within the poems, the untransformed Ego is occasionally referred to as Eve. In mythology Eve is Adam's second wife and is generally accepted as good/civilised.

The buried Goddess that needs reclaiming is known by different names according to the stage in the healing process: A voice crying in the wilderness, Abandoned child, A Lost Soul, A Reject, Virgin, and Lilith. In mythology Lilith is Adam's first wife and is generally considered bad/uncivilised.

In the narrative the conflict between Eve and Lilith is because they are opposites. Eve is conscious (ego) and Lilith exists in the unconscious.

Once united, I have named them Camilla Leon. This comes from a twist on the word chameleon, a lizard that has the capacity to change its appearance and transform, and as we all have the capacity to become whole, I use Camilla Leon as a symbol for 'everyone'.

Metaphors used

For Soul: The Butterfly and Dove

For Ego: Steed, Horse and Mount

For Consciousness: Life, River or Sea.

Space for Soul in waiting: Casket on the Island, Cocoon, and Cage.

Lilith is my middle name and I have referred to her in one of the poems as my hidden namesake.

Presentation of the Poems

So, now let us approach the poems to see how they are organised in order to convey the experience of the spiritual journey.

Preludes

There is a prelude prior to each new Cycle of Poems. The purpose of these is to inform you of my experience prior to the moment of beginning the new Cycle, including any trainings undertaken or important events. In this way you are invited to share my state of mind as I begin the new cycle in real time.

Three Cycles

There are three cycles of poems, each separated by a *Gap* in time. This was not a matter of choice, but was dictated by the spiritual process itself. A cycle is started when effort is put into the process of transformation and there is growth in awareness and maturity of the individual, achieved during the *Gap* Period. The commencement of a Cycle of Poems indicates that a harvest from such development is now ready for conscious assimilation via the poems.

The time taken to complete a cycle varies according to what has to be achieved, Cycle One took 24 years. Cycle Two took 17 years, including the *Interim Poems*, and Cycle Three took 3 years to complete. The reasons for this are described in Part Two.

The Erratic Nature of the Process of Change

Every transformational process has its ups and downs. To clarify this, imagine you are trying to kick a bad habit – let's choose something extreme to make the erratic nature of the process clearer, say drug abuse, alcoholism, gambling addiction etc. There is a **definite profile** to the stages one goes through in efforts to overcome such addictions.

Alchemical Stages

The **Alchemical Process** is one which recognises the erratic nature of any process of transformation and it incorporates this fact by establishing 8 stages which represent these ups and downs, which are clarified below.

Stage One: Awakening to present reality and recognising that changes need to be made.

Stage Two: Emotionally adjusting to the adaptations needed.

Stage Three: What to keep and what to jettison. Potential losses.

Stage Four: Head and heart agree on the changes needed. Harmony.

Stage Five: Dark night of the soul. Suffering experienced as changes **have not yet been made.** The suffering is a powerful incentive to make the changes.

Stage Six: Rallying of courage and determination to make the changes. Hope revives.

Stage Seven: Refining the progress made. Possible back-sliding, but you have the courage to resume your efforts.

Stage Eight: Celebrate the changes made, for this nourishes the continuing process.

Consciousness & Spiritual Transformation

The process of personal transformation is both difficult and challenging and tends to take a long time, but the highs and lows typical of all forms of transformation are also evident here.

The poems in a cycle reflect these stages, which is why each cycle of poems is separated into stages. The experiences of the journey are reflected in the tone and content of the poems at each stage.

Abbreviations Used

It is easy to lose track of which cycle and stage one is in, so I have used the following abbreviations should you wish to keep track. They are to be found at the top left-hand side, close to the poems title.

PoI = Poems of Innocence

Cycle = C and Stage = S. Thus, Cycle 2, Stage 6 = C2S6

Int.P = Interim Poems

Int.P, LC = Last Confessions

Int.P, RPE = Requiem for passing Era

C.S.J = Poems illustrating Challenges of the Spiritual Journey

Analysis

At the end of each cycle of poems is an analysis of the meaning of each poem. The early poems do not really need this as they are self-explanatory, but the later poems are more complicated and so I felt an analysis might be helpful.

Commentary

Knowing what each poem means in isolation gives no indication of the progress made. This only becomes apparent when the ground covered by the whole Cycle of Poems is considered. For this reason, there is a Commentary at the end of each Cycle of Poems.

POEMS Pre-CYCLE ONE

I had not heard from my inner voice since I was seven years old. Now after fourteen years she again broke into my consciousness. I came to call this inner voice my 'Muse' as she communicated with me through poems. At first there were a number of gentle poems about the beauty of nature and the joy of living, and these predisposed me to becoming more open to her presence in my life. I have entitled these five poems as 'Poems of Innocence' and I list them below. They are straight forward and need little comment.

POEMS OF INNOCENCE

Sky:	Wondering at the mystery of the sky.
To Freedom:	The desire to be at one with nature.
Joy in the Beauty of Nature:	Surrendering to the beauty of God's world.
Joy:	Intuiting and celebrating my oneness with the beauty of life.
Ecstasy of Freedom:	Ecstasy of being alive.

Pol

SKY

Sometimes I stand and look at you
A great expanse of crystal blue,
And I try to pierce the heart of you
To look beyond you, or look through.

And then I wonder what or who
Could half have dreamed, half thought of you.

But all at once comes into view
A little cloud, a bird or two

And once again, I see the hue.

1966

Pol

TO FREEDOM

Oh, to be alone with the wind
The warm west wind and I.
Together we'd sooth this troubled world
And banish clouds from the sky.

As one we'd race the stallion wild
Across some western plain,
And rock the bee in his bluebell bower
To warn him of pending rain.

From high above the pounding seas,
We'd swoop and skim the wave
And lash it into a fury
Fit to blanche the sailor brave.

On the back of the Eagle we'd take our rest,
As she circled and soared in the sky.
And the ponderous swish of those heavy wings
Would be our lullaby.

1965

Pol

JOY IN THE BEAUTY OF NATURE

I stand and look upon the view
Stretched panoramically before me,
And I'm filled with a boundless quivering joy
A trembling love and affinity.

A cool fresh flush of air sweeps away
The cobwebs of careless perception,
And with crystalline gaze I discern
The beauty in God's creation.

The sun shines warm on my upturned face
And gleams amber through my eyelid screen.
The gentle breeze caresses my cheek
And tempts with the perfume of flowers unseen.

1967

'Magnolias'

Pol

JOY

The biting thrill of sparkling thistles
Dressed in tears of morning dew,
Scorching rays of lime and crimson
A searing flash of cobalt blue,
Bound together with jewels of water
Crystal life of every hue.
Liquid love which shines with laughter
Coursing life through tender veins,
Swells to fullness seeds of springtime
Fruit of joy and love and rain.

Am I here just to see you?
And feel the joy you have for life?
Or is it you who are for me?
Or are we one?

1969

Pol

ECSTASY OF FREEDOM

A kick in my stomach like fear,
A thrill in my nerves like pain,
A fire and a joy in my heart
Which suffuses, confuses the brain.
Short sharp breaths coming quickly,
Eager heart, eager soul, eager eyes,
That yearn to the far horizon
And drown in overwhelming skies.

19.01.1969

PART ONE

The Spiritual Journey

Chapter One

Cycle One: A Lost Soul Seeking Direction

PRELUDE TO CYCLE ONE

These early poems were rarely dated, simply filed under the decade they were written and numbered according to their position in the file. I kept this system in creating the poem lists, for it makes it clear that the poems were consecutive and their appearance within a particular Stage of the Cycle is not arbitrary. However, it is the meaning of the poem which determines which Stage in the Cycle it belongs to and this occasionally interrupts the strictly consecutive order of the poems.

It was not until the 1990's that I began to date each poem and this appears on the poem itself.

I was deeply unhappy, frustrated and disillusioned prior to entering Cycle One. I had studied sciences with the hope of becoming a doctor but this was not an option, so instead I worked in Medical Research as a technician. I anticipated the work would result in solutions to human illnesses, but the tasks I had to undertake were either repellent to me involving experiments on animals, or were mind-numbingly boring. I was ready to change directions in my life. I was twenty-one.

Once the First Cycle began the poems had a very different quality to the Poems of Innocence.

POEMS SELECTED FOR CYCLE ONE

My Files

Stage One:	5 poems	Change	1960's	No. 5
		The Question	60's	No. 7
		Wondering	60's	No. 11
		Loss of Clear Vision	60's	No. 14
		The Easy Way	60's	No. 22
Stage Two:	5 poems	Loneliness	60's	No. 12
		No End to Living	1970's	No. 4
		Broken	70's	No. 5
		The Courage to Respond	70's	No. 8
		Fear of Freedom	70's	No. 16
Stage Three:	3 poems	Gift Love not Need Love	1980's	No. 1
		Solace	80's	No. 2
		Death of a Friend	80's	No. 4
Stage Four:	3 poems	I Love the Night	80's	No. 3
		Precious Friend	80's	No. 5
		Falling into Love	80's	No. 6
Stage Five:	4 poems	Barren	80's	No. 7
		Sterile	80's	No. 8
		A Gift of Love	80's	No. 10
		The Virgin	80's	No. 13
Stage Six:	2 poems	How Do you Do it?	80's	No. 9
		The Power of Love	80's	No. 12
Stage Seven:	5 poems	The Eye of the Demon Queen	80's	No. 17
		Lilith	1990's	No. 2
		Rejection of a female Therapist	90's	No. 6
		Death Wish	90's	No. 7
		Fear Grows, Defences Unravel	90's	No. 11
Stage Eight:	3 poems	To Touch God	1991	
		Need	16.12.1992	
		The Goddess	21.12.1992	
Total:	30 poems			

C1S1

CHANGE

Sometimes my life eludes me.
The shifting merging scenes evaporate
And nebulous expanses of feeling
Disperse any constancy or shape.

The tiny wisps of reality
Which I thought so stolidly real,
Dance and fluctuate like shadows
Fading to illusions I can't feel.

Let them go, then come again
Familiar ghosts of phantasy.
It's comforting to recognise a dream
No need to fix it perpetually.

What I though was concrete
Has changed with time's strange alchemy.
I hold to nought, should it remain
No doubt I'd change and need to wander free.

1968/69

C1S1

THE QUESTION

I look hard at my life!
It disintegrates before me
Into fragments of mundane activity.

What is life?
Where in this myriad of notions,
Creation, sensations, emotions
Is life?

I look back over the years
And try to find in experience
Some fundamental principle
The logic of my existence.

Familiar dear faces and bloody wars,
Sunshine, laughter and sparkling seas
Raw nerves twitching and open sores
Festering and weeping in the stagnant breeze.

No! This isn't what I'm looking for,
This chronicle of historical fact.
Where is the power, the purpose, the core
The one unknown in every act?

Sadly I watched the visions fade,
Tormented by a sense of frustration.
If this is all there is to life
What is the point of creation?

1968

C1S1

WONDERING

And so I sit here wondering
What the years will bring to me.
Will I fulfil my dearest ambitions
Or die in conformity?

Will the fates be kind and bless my endeavours
Raining sweetly upon the root?
Or will the dice be against me forever
To embitter the taste of the fruit?

How easy it would be to accept each day
Without effort or dreams or ambition,
To meet the demands passed on the way
Without thought to a purpose or mission.

But how sad too, if we lose the zest
Which inspires and shapes our lives.
Which precludes us from giving less than our best
On which all achievement thrives.

For it's only by effort and bitter contention
We attain full maturity,
Only then can we know the nature of freedom
And have life more abundantly.

1968

C1S1

LOSS OF A CLEAR VISION

And so I stare it blandly in the face,
This garish pageantry of days and years
And try, by staring out my fears
To find some truth.

But as I stare, I lose without a trace
This vision clear and watch through baffled tears
The scene contort and twist. Naught interferes
But my own thoughts, which give each other chase.
It is not well to look too hard at life.

1968

C1S1

THE EASY WAY ?

I really try to lose myself
In everyday affairs,
In rigid blind performance
To drown these haunting cares,
But what is life if all our time
Is spent in repressing ourselves,
And our dreams are pleasant fantasies
We obediently shelve?

I think I could learn to be content
In this dull mechanical way,
If my cherished hopes would not flare up
And burn my blindness away.

01.08.1968

C1S2

LONELINESS

My very soul cries out to God
Against the depth of this misery,
This drear and weary joyless state
Of suffocating anonymity.

I look around, everywhere I see
People laughing in the joy of life,
Whilst within my own oppressed soul
Like a cankerous worm, breeds strife.

I see the things that once gave me joy
And caused my loving heart to sing,
But the lonely heart they cannot soothe
Only mock and scorch and sting.

I pass through life like a ghost of myself
Only here in solitude am I real,
For though I long to express myself
I cannot communicate what I feel.

For all the joy and fire and zest
That once seemed to pound in my veins,
That filled my heart with unspeakable joy
And flashed inspiration into my brain,

Has withered like a parched flower
Grown listless and ugly in the scorching sun.
All effort seems a pointless thing
And the fruits – not worthy to be won.

1967-68

C1S2

NO END TO LIVING

Sometimes, like now, it seems impossible.
Why should I have to keep on fighting?
The will to push on further seems to die.
Let me stop, let me sleep, let me die.

I'm sure this can't be right.
The life which should be flowing freely
Is all damned up, bound fast and tight.

There seems no end to living.

1970's

C1S2

BROKEN

Nasty jagged spiteful little splinters
Which tear and rip and charge with pain
How efficiently you make me scream and tremble
And wrench the bloody anguished tears away.

What have I done to you?
What evil sin so vilely committed?
What omnipotent natural law
Transgressed against?
I wish I knew.

I look within myself
To try and find some clue.
I thought I understood
Yet somehow I've done wrong
And must accept the consequences.

Perhaps I have ignored
The gentle warnings,
The tender hints
Which tried to point the way.

But now I'm smashed and
Sorely, souly broken.
They dare me now
To say I have not heard.

1970's

C1S2

THE COURAGE TO RESPOND

Oh for the strength to just stand firm
And not duck out next time that life draws near.
To stand erect and face to face,
Identify the question.

And trembling still from the shock
Of violated vulnerability,
Fulfil the obligation
Implicit in that time.

Rise uncertainly and painfully
And straining up with frightened heart
Try to respond, drawn by the surging
Floods of life which leap
In answer to the call.

1970's

C1S2

FEAR OF FREEDOM

The fine dividing line
Between chaos and order
We tread with care,
And blot out the proximity
Of anarchy with frantic action,
Self-imposed and clutched at.
Erected out of self-inflicted social norms
We call our duty, obligation, what you will.

Not what *I* will,
That's too intensely real a question
To dignify with recognition.
Instead, we cling to actions
Which we fool ourselves
Are imposed on us
By our society.

Afraid to let them go,
To face ourselves and
The terror of free will and choice
Which freedom thus implies.

We glimpse the hovering void which begs decision,
And terror-filled plunge back into a fixed identity,
Massively relieved that we can hide ourselves,
And slumber heavily amidst the solid web
Of social inter-weavings.
Oblivious to the throbbing mass of life
We are too weak to dare.

For life is vast and strange,
Anonymous, but there.
Our refuge from the confrontation?
The anaesthetic that we call our duty.
The barricade behind which we grovel stupidly.
And all events which could give life a meaning
We hide from and wilfully reject our destiny,

Preferring to huddle aimlessly in stupid hoards,
The weight and size of which
Drag down our hopes and dreams,
Till they are trampled in the mud
Beneath the feet of
Cowardly normality.

The smell and brutish warmth we thus obtain
Are regarded as a bargain,
At the expense of freedom
And individual destiny.

1970's

C1S3

GIFT LOVE - NOT NEED LOVE

How I long for you.
To be encompassed by your loving,
Cocooned within the warmth of caring,
Nourished by your loving acceptance
Of what I am.

Not approval – but joyous recognition
And the blessed holy cherishing
And succour of all that is life furthering,
Promoting and nurturing
All that is most beautiful
Within my struggling soul.

And yet I know, were I to live
Within the shelter of your blessed love,
I would not venture more.
I would have, here and now,
Externally provided
That which I have to learn to generate.

Surrounded by your boundless love out there,
What need then to strive and stretch
And grow in my ability to love?

I still need to face and feel unmitigated
The pain arising from my childish dependence.

I want love – bestowed upon me from without.
My mother's milk, my father's approval.
Yet till I have outgrown these needs,
Till I have learnt to generate myself
The love within I seek so desperately out there,
I am not ready to respond
In all my glorious wholeness
To the beauty that you are.

Someday, maybe,
When you and I have grown,

When we can meet
Without clinging and losing ourselves
In a symbiosis of mutual love
Which excludes all but us.

When each of us has learned to be the love we seek,
Then maybe we can meet again.
And having become our separate selves,
Be twice as powerful.
Each stimulating and nourishing
The other's ability to generate love.

With pooled resources of loving,
We could, between us
Generate a child of love,
That might transfigure this world.

27.06.1982

C1S3

SOLACE

I pass the little houses,
Fascinated yet repelled.
I know the life that goes on there
Behind those glowing windows,
Demurely draped – bland boredom.

I do not want to enter there,
Participate in their predictable rituals,
The hemmed in sanity,
Which proclaims its basic fear.

And yet I do get solace
From looking at their homes,
As a sailor out to sea
Finds comfort in
Familiar landmarks.

16.05.1983

C1S3

DEATH OF A FRIEND

Live and let die, so says the song.
Let go, allow the dead to go their way.

How sad – how transient,
How irrevocable it seems.
Dear friend, will I never see you again?

Somehow it all seems pointless.
You seemed so strong,
A fundamental bastion of my life
And now – you're gone.

I miss you dear friend.
You weren't my mother – but dear,
And knowing you – and missing you
Bequeaths a timely warning,
To love those close to you
While you have them.
They too could die tomorrow
With unmerciful finality.

Take every opportunity
To love and show that love.
Don't hope it may be guessed at
Beneath your hard demeanour.

Allow that love to shine
So fully, unmistakably and clearly
That when the time for parting comes
There are no unexpressed emotions,
No regrets for things not said.

To each person in my life
I'll give all the love I can.
I'll generate and spend
All my life in loving.

For when all is said and done
What else has meaning?
What else relieves the heartache
Except the memory of love shared?

I don't believe you are no more.
I believe with all my heart
You still survive somewhere,
Yet – how long until I see you?

I send you love my friend,
Love to smooth the way for you.
I'm sad you are gone.
I'll miss you.

May 1983

C1S4

I LOVE THE NIGHT

I love the night.
Sweet anonymity,
When I can wander aimlessly and free.
No enquiring glances or hostile stares
To violate my openness – my nakedness.
I can weep or hum or stop and stare,
No-one to mark the strangeness of my mood
Or avoid me out of fear.

I walk and walk
And smell the open universe about me,
Cool – impersonal – yet secure.
For whatever I am – it encloses,
Requiring nought – sufficient – steady
Implacable, but there.

I feel accepted here – in night space,
Where street lights emphasise the emptiness
And silence comforts me – invisibly.
No need to talk – bridge spaces in between,
For here I feel my inmost soul transparent
Perceived – and recognised.

Mute life, which tries to tear apart this vessel
In order to escape – be one with you,
Need I slit myself from throat to bowel
And tear apart the gaping wound
To let this inside enter space –
Share itself – be manifest?

Not in the quiet space of night,
For here there is no 'me'.
Just one extended life.

16.05.1983

C1S4

PRECIOUS FRIEND

A precious friend.
Experiences and life we've shared.

I love you,
I want you in my life.
Let little things like
Wives and girl friends
Take their place.

I need you.
You are a matrix.
Much stronger than emotion,
You form a background to my life.

I love you.
Please don't abandon me.

I love you.
Don't forget me.

Today we met again.
So long since we were together,
But you are part of me,
Part of my past,
Part of my life,
Part of me.

I see you today,
Yet you are full of yesterdays for me.

I met your father once,
I loved your mother – dearly,
And I am meshed with you
From holidays and ventures,
I love you.

I don't live with you.
Don't make love with you,

Yet when we meet
It's nourishment so full,
So full of feeling for me.

I want to see you happy,
Centred,
Loved and fulfilled.
I love you.

Remember –
We always can remember,
So easily.
We use a language
Long since outgrown today
But appropriate.

You speak to me in words I know.
People we've met,
Things we have done,
Memories we've shared,
Oh, how I love you.

Don't let small jealousies
Separate us.
Love is too precious,
Love like our knowing
Our common language.

You always seem to know
Just what I need to grow
And say it.

I love you.

1986

C1S4

FALLING INTO LOVE

And so I hold my breath,
And humbly, silently watch
A miracle – in birth.
Magic swelling slowly,
Unmistakably,
Within my breast.
A warmth, a joy,
The birth pangs of an ecstasy.

Too much to see – I close my eyes.
Pretend I do not see,
For fear my brutal gaze will harm it.

Like a tiny tender leaf
That's just unfurling,
Don't touch it or disturb it.
Pretend I have not seen it.
Any tender touch of mine
May be too rough,
Prove too strong
And make it shrink away.

Like a dream, surprised on waking,
That subtly changes form and disappears.
Irretrievably lost, the flavour gone,
Receding further
As I strain to bring it back.

Will this too change and fade away?
So delicate, so new,
So strange and beautiful.
So welcome, yet so utterly beyond
My power to control.

A dream, pulsating into life.

1986

C1S5

BARREN

Dear Heart
I love you so much.

In my mind's eye I see you
With your woman and your children,
And I die a little.

You love me – I know it,
Yet there is some part of you – apart.

I see you playing with your children.
Their ecstatic whoops of joy,
Their little clinging arms around your neck,
Your joy reflecting theirs in fun and play.
I love to see you thus – in my mind's eye.

Yet in reality, I'm also sad.
I too would like to play with them,
Enjoy their little skinny arms around my neck,
Play foolish pranks – swap silly jokes
And love each other,
Easily.

Oh, how I envy you this part,
How excluded from this family I feel,
And what can I – a barren woman – give?

It hurts.
To know I'll never be complete –
A barren woman……..

Yet, I could conceive – it is by choice.
Somehow the longing is too weak,
I fear I could not love enough.
For other offspring of my heart and mind and soul
Consume my energy,
None left to nurture children.

And so, I cry – to realise
I always shall be barren.

And though my soul
May print itself among the stars,
And should I realise
Other dreams and fantasies,
Somehow, I'll know
I failed.

For you I never was all woman.
We never touched that height,
We never made a life together.

So, I am grateful to your other woman,
You're spared the pain of being barren.

1986

C1S5

STERILE

God! – It's evil.
As soon as I dared to feel again
The eruption started.
Quivers deep deep down.
Heat – trickling slowly up into my frozen body.
Cheeks starting to warm, then tingle,
Then pulse heavily, with rage,
So heavily subdued till now.

I left them an hour ago,
Those sweet nice civilised corpses,
And breathed the joyous breath
Of one who had feared suffocation.

And I felt the impulses flash,
The ones I'd noticed, but studiously ignored,
Suppressed – staved off – till it was safe to own them.

The burning hatred of sterility.
For that is what it is.
A sterile, barren, stale-mate situation,
In which each side loses constantly.

A barren collusion.
A yielding out of misguided loyalty.
A quick placation,
To avoid head on collision.
My God – it stinks.

And they wonder why we are sterile!
It's a wonder we survived,
And perverse, spiteful, cruel I feel
Because I can no longer be a cipher.

I can no longer pretend I feel their way.
I see their acts as anti-life and evil.
They avoid the head on collision
That their two honesties require,

And they hedge and dance and yield
Out of fear of loneliness.

I cannot play their game,
Yet I cannot be myself.
Instead, a gradual dying in their presence.
A sharp withdrawal,
Which slowly becomes complete
Till I am there in body only.

I wish I did not love them,
For it's that which hooks me in.
I wish I would be honest
And confront them
With their self-earned isolation.

They made us sterile
And then proceed to lament their fate!
No grandchildren around,
How fruitless can we be?
How cruel.

No grandchildren to reward their care of us.
God!
They made us sterile
And we're to take the blame?

26.07.1986

'Projection then Reflection'

C1S5

A GIFT OF LOVE

I fell.
Cold, Frozen, Stone.
Deathlike, Spaceless Void,
Spiked.
Painfully searing me awake.
Heavy, hated duration – escape to sleep and sleep
Escape abysmal spaces.
Abysmal, dismal, pain filled day.
Fly to massive densities of sleep.

And then – explosion,
In slow, slow motion,
Of blackness – evil – putrid,
Uncoiling lividly – scarlet slashes searing through.
Unrolling foetid masses – spreading menace.

Crackling then – spitting fires of rage.
A ragged rent – volcanic heavings,
Spewing out a putrid, glabrous, oozing mass.
Enraged.
Frustrated fury – hatred – silent screaming terror,
Building fast, till bursting in my brain
It spread its venom straight into my mind
And body, heart, guts seething
Vilely embroiled.
A bloody sulphurous infusion –
Life giving – *cauterising viciously*
The unknown wound.

Round and round it poured,
And burst and scalded, searing black.
Hatred crashing endlessly within my head.
Rage beating at my heart and lungs.
Get out and kill, smash, pulverise –
Hate gone mad.
Round and round – pulverising cells,
Boiled, scalded, screaming.

Slowly.......................the power flagged – slowly.
So slowly ebbing,
And only spiteful fantasies flared up
Intermittently.
And a grim, bitter, torpid pain began to grow.
A sickness – revulsion – aversion.
Withdrawing silently within – Against it –
The cause – the hated thing.

Two days of sickness – retching feelings in the gut,
Heart, lungs and belly full of rancid rage,
Turning to bile and pain.
A pain which suffused each cell and nerve –
Which mounted – to my throat –
Pressing hard and painfully –
Excruciating clamour for release.

Stop feeling – Just to stop feeling.
I'll give away my feeling birth-right,
I did before.
But now I've gone too far –
I started this – there is no turning back.
So, I ferment slowly

Time passes.

And then I see I can say "go away" to it.
And relief floods in.
I can choose not to see it
And for one false second, I turn away
And close my eyes
And pretend I can have none of it,
I can refuse to see.

And then a clear, silent space.
No pain. But peace.
And from that grace –
I chose to own it
The hated thing....is mine....me
The bit.......I chose....not to see.

And as I owned it – it fell away from you.
And I ached with love and gratitude.
You took a risk – unknowingly.
In love or hate –
You held the mirror up for me.

I shuddered – how ugly you are
Until I recognised.......

The rage and fury, pain despair.......
Resistances – and features.
The acid bit through
My frightened, screwed-up eyelids
And I saw
And recognised....Me.

How can you bear to look at me.

1986

C1S5

THE VIRGIN

I remember how it felt,
So cold – alone on that pedestal
Upon which I balanced,
Precariously.

Marble – cold – dead,
Like an unresponsive prick.

I am worshipped and feared,
Mocked, hated and adored,
Yet never loved.

As virgin I am pure,
Above the needs of the flesh
Until I shattered.

I screamed and fought my way
Off that fucking pedestal.
The terror of being
The focus of so much hate.

The men, they either mocked,
And tried their damnedest
To knock me off,
And if I fell – they jeered
And hate filled,
Trampled me underfoot,
Screaming hate – slut – whore.

But had I stayed there
Cold – alone – abandoned,
And taken the weight of their
Hypocritical adoration?
It smothered me,
It dragged me down with a
Weight of grief I could not bear.

And – so – I paid the price
Of having offended?
I cast aside that false treasure
I thought I'd been protecting.

I looked about and picked
A man I knew was love-sick,
Rid myself of the guarded prize,
For then at least, I could get down.
Could topple off that pedestal.

From there, I made my way
Haltingly, to some far distant goal.
I knew I would know it
Once I got there.

I had to learn to walk,
The pedestal requires immobility,
A death like stance
Of purity.

And when I fell – No!
I did it purposely.
And when *I* chose,
Not being forced by them,
I chose the spot I fell in
And paid my dues.

And long, long did it take me
And much blood and tears
To learn to walk – naturally.

At last I got there,
Found the destination
I'd seen from the pedestal,
Only to find,
An immobile was wanted,
Being able to walk
Disqualified me.

It sounds like bitterness,
Yet hurts, a deep-down pain.
A grief – I dare not own
For it will splinter me.

I believed their values,
And now, having found my own
Through trial and error,
Learned just too late
That I was right,
And they were wrong.

It doesn't help,
To know I'm right.
Just adds a bitterness
To pain.

The pain of my self-betrayal.
It's just that I could hear them,
They were bigger than me,
Had louder voices.

And when I had grown up
And learned to hear my own,
It was too late.

25.11.1986

C1S6

HOW DO YOU DO IT?

How do you do it?
Put your finger so precisely on the spot
The wound most people do not see.
Un-phased by your knowledge
Of the fragility approached,
Compassionately seeking,
Always the meaning,
The significance.

And even as I flinch,
Longing to evade this brutal exploration,
I'm fascinated.
Your insistence captivates me,
Commands an equal honesty,
Demands a truthfulness to you
A level of respect I rarely grant,
Except to God, sometimes myself.
A profound power that has to be evoked.

I see I cannot get away
With unrevealing vagaries.
The blunt, raw, unrefined facts,
As far as I can dig them out,
Is what you want.

I do not need to patronise you,
Or protect you from the truth
I feel you may not understand.
Nor insult you with crude messages,
Which do not tell, but veil the truth.
I cannot, out of laziness,
Or an underestimation of your need to know,
Evade your point.

For in that directness,
You are yourself revealed.
I see a drive for truth

That touches me so deeply
I love you more
And know that I can trust it.

1986

C1S6

THE POWER OF LOVE

Is it not enough that I love you?
Is it not enough that I share
All I know how?
Is it not enough that I put everything
I can, into our space?

You wallow in your swamp
Flailing wildly,
Attempting half heartedly
To get out.

And you hate me.
You want me in that swamp with you.
You want me filthy, degraded, deranged,
A filthy bag of shit you can relate to,
A hellish mate you can feel equal to.

Like a short-sighted fool,
Complaining that the world is too small.
You can't value anything,
Can't see anything
Not stained with shit.

Your currency is shit.
You know the value of it
It's richness, a compost
From which orchids grow.

But they are too beautiful,
Too sweet, too fresh and lovely,
Smelling sweet, not shitty.
You can't value them,
Their currency is shitless.

Must I jump in too?
And wallow like you
Complaining of the stench?

You want blood and power.
Slit myself from cunt to mouth
And let my guts fall out
Into the swamp?
We can compare out innards.

"Where are you ?" you scream,
"Where are your guts?
Where's your blood and pain and shit?"
And ignore the fact
I'm trying hard to pull you out.

There is a space here, I'm holding onto,
Fighting for, sweating fear,
That you will pull me in.
But you prefer the swamp,
Demand that if I love you
I prove it, jump in and wallow too.

You bastard.
And you say you love me!
Who then will pull me out?

You have a choice,
The swamp – in or out?
But don't expect me to come in.

For that's not evidence of love,
It's suicide.

_____

I remember the time I crawled out of the swamp,
It took eternity.
I had been told it was the way to go.
I was seeking love and that was the way to go.
I clambered, clawed and fought to make my way,
My fingers bled.

Each time I turned and saw the swamp still there,
Warm and inviting, full of familiar nightmares.
It looked benign – comforting.

Full of hellish bedfellows
Who were at least familiar,
And I sweated fear
And tasted horror.

Terror made me stretch myself,
To climb the bank
And struggle out.

And love beckoned me.
For love alone could bear to wait.
Only love could bear to see my fear,
Could lovingly extend a hand,
Could watch my agony,
Be with my pain,
Receive my hate,
And smiling still
Hold out a hand and beckon me.

And needing, wanting love so much,
I struggled and bent my back and will and soul
To reach the outstretched hand.

At last, I made it,
And crouched, shivering and naked,
Cold and filthy, by the swamp,
Getting used to the altitude.

And rain came, of tears, and washed me,
And the sun of love – it warmed me,
And slowly I stood up – to look for love,
The goal that I had striven for.

And gently – I was turned around.
In disbelief – I recognised
That love was there, where I had been.
Love – in you – was struggling in the swamp,
Blindly straining – seeking love and freedom.

So, I held out my hand.
How much I need you on the bank with me.

For seeking love – is being love.
I'm waiting – loving you –
I've fought to reach you,
By climbing out the swamp.
All along, I've been seeking you.

And now it is my turn,
And I hold out my hand and beckon you
And hope my love is adequate.

When you are here with me,
We can go on together.

Late 1986

C1S7

THE EYE OF THE DEMON QUEEN

The orb – her eye,
Look in – drown deeply – deeper in
And release, surrender, yield.

Allow the grand dissolution of illusion.
Release control – overflow false limits,
Allow – increase – become fecund and spacious.
Flow – generously out. Endlessly spilling life,
Falling, loving, cascades of living light, nascent energy.

Demonic?   No.   But Awe-full.

1980's

C1S7

LILITH

Are you my Lilith?
Harsh figure barring my way to love,
Black angel with flaming sword,
Eyes black and fiery red.

The only way to pass you
Is by loving you.

To love you – I need to know you.
Why do you bar my way?

Is there a meaning I can understand?

15.10.1990

C1S7

REJECTION OF A FEMALE THERAPIST

It was 'her' who tricked me in the first place.
'She' who betrayed me – taught me to betray myself.

Should I now open up myself to 'her' intervention
When she has proved how untrustworthy 'she' is?

Suppose I did – and she 'helped' me.
I won't do it.
I would have to be grateful to 'her'
I would then be affirming 'her'.
If I do that – I am saying it was okay.
Okay to teach me how to betray myself.

As a child – I felt I was sparing her.
By keeping my pain to myself
And not sharing it,
I was sparing her my pain.

But now I see, it was myself I was sparing.
I did not trust her.
She would have used my pain
Against me.

The Ultimate 'She'.
Until I find one I can trust
How can I live my 'she-ness'?

Funny, I thought it was a 'bargain' struck.
No – not a bargain,
Not even a compromise,
But a 'con' – I was cheated.

The adaptive child behaves the way it does
In order to survive – but what survives?
Only an adapted child.

14.08.1992

C1S7

DEATH WISH

Can I forgive myself for betraying me?
Or do I hate myself so much for that
That I would rather die?

A bargain struck – so I thought,
I would give myself away
But they – in turn – would give me back,
So, what went wrong?

Betrayed I was, betrayed I am.
They taught me
How to betray myself,
And I learnt it well.

They don't have to bother any more.
I do it to myself.

To myself?
Or what is left of me.

My rage and shame and anger,
All bottled up
Till I am sick of feeling
And cease to feel.

Despair is what is left.
I might as well finish it,
Finish what they started.

14.08.1992

C1S7

FEAR GROWS AS MY DEFENCES UNRAVEL

Shell-shocked. She said I looked shocked.
Fear – I really did not want to go back
To that place that loomed – threatening me.
The menace of it. I feel deeply afraid
Of the effects I have felt within.

I have begun to unravel – relax.
My habitual defences,
Not even recognised as such,
Below my awareness level,
Staunch allies of my sanity
Began to melt, disintegrate.

And between the fissures and cracks
Of that strong edifice, fear leached through,
Like the pale blue smoke of a fire
Long since extinguished – or thought so.
That slender fragile tremulous wisp of blue
Betraying a rekindled passion –
A fire not dead at all –
In wait, biding its time,
Like a predatory beast, waiting, to pounce
Upon its unsuspecting prey.

So long I have controlled it.
Been strong – banished it – or so I thought
And yet I recognise the smell
Of fear. The caustic tendrils
Which undermine foundations.

An underground river,
Which feeds tributaries of corrosion,
That eat into the footings
And decimate, erode, breakdown – me.

That hints at the fear – the terror deep down
Of my own worthlessness.

It is not a concept – it's a feeling,
Of being...............a reject.
Not a fear of being seen as one.
The ice-olating knowledge – I am one.
Like tendrils of weakness –
Leaching through my body,
Sapping everything else.
My life, strength, neutralised by fear.

Rejection – fuels it.
Confirms my self-perception.

I need to be rejected,
For that feeds my sense of being real.

I am a reject.
So if you don't reject me –
You invalidate me.

I force your rejection, to confirm myself.

You must suffer me,
For my reality
Is to be under sufferance.

You must relate to me – as I feel myself,
Or else you undermine the rock
On which I'm built.
The rock of self-hatred, self denial, self-less-ness.

To confirm myself,
To value myself,
How can I?
All I can do – is cover up – deny
Resist with love the knowledge
That I am a reject.

And tasting now – this feeling
Familiar – rejected – disowned,
Of being tolerated,
Of living under sufferance.

Abandoned.
What did I do
That was so bad?

Just living?
Was that my fault?

Yet I have paid for it
Each hour,
And tried so hard to forget
Distance the knowing.

Like something evil, deformed,
Putrid – crawling from a swamp.
How come they let me live,
Why?
It would have been kinder
To let me die.

And black hatred
For all that pain.
Damn you to hell
Where I have been so long.

Forgive you?
I have yet to feel the hate in full.
Ask again –
Then.

October 1992

C1S8

TO TOUCH GOD

To touch inside – connect – ground myself in being.
So much activity – Externally directed –
I want to formulate myself – initiate myself,
Plug into that inner realm of fantasy – of feeling,
Of dreams and play.

The inner stream – of many coloured shapes and shades
And endless possibilities – a rainbow river
Of longings and vaguely felt aspirings.
How to plug in?
How to begin to grasp Ariadne's thread?

To unravel deftly – a continuously arising
String of novelties – that leave banality behind,
That flee prosaic meanings and begin to express
Through awkward phrases and stumbled words,
To indicate, implicate, evoke and arbitrate
Another world behind, beyond, within.

Keep trying – keep reaching out.
It is the world behind these words I want to reach,
Yet somehow – the words become the very barrier
To expressing what I wish to say.

The world of dreams,
Of fluid forms – dissolving into others.
Of meaning scarcely held before it
Shades into others – many – contrariwise
And similar and opposite and other.

Life itself – I want to grasp, to know it.
Not in all its various modes and forms
And qualities – for those are limitless.

It's the essence I want.
To grasp it, taste it, feel it,
Be awe struck by its power.

Too much mediocrity – too much banality.
I want to taste life's inscrutability,
Drown in its otherness and magic.

Blossom in forests of weirdness,
Expand beyond all predictability,
Be the potential,
Not savour just hints and passing phantoms.

To do something – right now –
That marks this moment.
Make of it, for me, something real,
Unique, to be remembered.

So many hours – each day –
Consumed in meaningless activity.
How Dare I!
To squander this priceless gift of life
In what! A struggle to survive?

I could spend my whole life
Just staying alive – never living.
I'm wasting a potential,
A magnificent trust is being squandered.

Yet it is through banality,
Through the very tedium we try to avoid
That great love expresses itself most clearly.

To touch God.
Transcend my limitations.
A hunger for the absolute and infinite.

The thin veil of contingencies
I want to rip it down.
Tear away the frail appearances
That mask vast powers
And awful presences.

1991

C1S8

NEED

Give a name to it –
The evil thing.

I think it is need,
Need to be loved.

An impossibility – I guess – to my mother.

And nobody else counted then.

So I learnt to experience myself as that –
Impossible to love.

What wonder then – I hate myself,
Discount and sabotage all that is me.

And **KNOW** I can't expect
Acceptance.

I pre-empt acceptance
By rejecting myself.

No wonder – I cannot allow myself success – happiness.

No wonder I fear intimacy – it courts rejection.

You cannot do anything else **but** reject a reject.

_____

Can I formulate, encapsulate that bit of me
So I *can* relate to it, sanctify it with my love
And heal the ravenous need?

Feed her the love she needs – so she can grow
Transform – become beloved?

16.12.1992

C1S8

THE GODDESS

A door has swung open.
I don't know how or why,
But simply now, I can step through.
It has revealed an inner room,
A crypt which holds my 'self'
A holy place where 'she' is at last revealed.

Not just to see – but be.
As if a final battlement has been breached
And I stand in awe of an unsuspected queen,
Seated – waiting for this moment.

She claims my obedience,
My allegiance, my love, my all.
That part of me that has waited
In gentle resignation – till I should turn
And see her, feel her, know her,
And at last yield to her claim.

A queen she is, a goddess
With power to heal my wounds.
I feel her claim and bow my head,
Ready to accede to her, hear and obey
Await her rule, a joy to serve.

A part of me – so long apart.
Why? I do not know.
She has been here forever.
I heard her – tapping on the inside of my soul
But did not know where to find it.

It has been there – this door – a long time.
I thought it was a prison door
That should be left locked.

Always I have revered the King,
Given him my service,
Listened for his command,

Assumed he had the right to rule,
And banish his forgotten Queen.

But all along she has been there,
Waiting – for me to arrive,
Waiting – till my knowledge of her dawned
And I would turn to her,
Astonished by her presence
So long unknown.

And my heart, so long entranced,
Fettered by harsh laws
Is freed, to follow its own path.
So soft and gentle, allegiance to love.
Fear put aside, obedience in joy.
A river following its destiny.

I did not understand
Why my heart was closed.
I heard the King command
Obeyed with mind – and body,
Yet my soul was not involved.
Somehow, 'I' was not inspired
Left cold, untouched, asleep.

And now, I have awakened
To a new day – new possibilities.
Excitement, so long dead,
Begins to build – joy to slowly dawn.
It will take time
For this bud to blossom,
And it grows in ecstasy.

And when I dress myself
And beautify my hair, my clothes,
It is not vanity. It never was.
Yet when I was estranged from her
How could I know
It was for her I dressed.

It was a form of worship

Of reverence, of praise.

A celebration and a joyful song
A 'Her' and not a 'Hymn'

A sacrifice to beauty,
Another of her names.
Beauty, Truth and Love she's called
In each of these I train.

21.12.1992

CYCLE ONE

ANALYSIS OF POEMS & THEIR MEANINGS

A Lost Soul Seeking Direction

Stage 1

'Change'

Awareness of the fluidity of both life and my sense of self.

'The Question'

Seeking for some meaning and purpose to my life.

'Wondering'

Recognising that true freedom has to be worked for.

'Loss of Clear Vision'

Desire to penetrate the surface of life to a deeper reality.

'The Easy Way'

Discontentment with an inauthentic life, revealed by flashes of inspiration.

Stage 2

'Loneliness'

Alienation and misery at the barrenness of life without love.

'No End to Living'

The exhaustion and despair of fighting one's defences against life.

'Broken'

The extreme suffering caused by unconscious emotional conflicts.

'The Courage to Respond'

Overcoming the fear and resistance to living authentically.

'Fear of Freedom'

We prefer the safety of conformity to freedom and thus lose our birth-right and purpose.

Stage 3

'Gift Love not Need Love'

Settling for need love keeps one a child. The capacity for gift love comes with wholeness.

'Solace'

Comforted by the signs of habitation, but alienated from that way of life.

'Death of a Friend'

Express the love you have for others now. It is too late once they are dead.

Stage 4

'I Love the Night'

Alone, walking at night, I feel safe, embraced by the kinship of life.

'Precious Friend'

The preciousness of long-standing friendships.

'Falling into Love'

Watching love blossom, secretly.

Stage 5

'Barren'

Acknowledging my pain that we will not share the joy of creating a child together, and gratitude to the mother of his children, who shared with him one of life's greatest gifts and spared him the pain of being barren.

'Sterile'

Revulsion at the conventions and collusions in relationships that suffocate authentic being.

'A Gift of Love'

This poem is about the devastating impact, physically, mentally, emotionally and spiritually when I became conscious that I had been locating my negativity and faults onto someone else and then judging them for these failings.

 If we withdraw those projections from the other person we see them for who they really are and can then do something about our own failings. (See the Commentary for a fuller understanding of this process.)

'The Virgin'

The soul's pain at its betrayal through ignorance, yet truth, though painful, is ultimately healing.

Stage 6

'How do you do it?'

A ruthless demand for unmitigated honesty in all its rawness is what you ask/need of me and I trust and honour this.

'The Power of Love'

Love was what released me from the mire of self-hatred, pulled me out of its clutches and healed me. Now it is my turn to live that love for you.

Stage 7

'The Eye of the Demon Queen'

We rejected her – called her demonic. We must surrender to her for she alone can make us whole.

'Lilith'

My Shadow blocks my path. I need to know, own her and love her to move on.

'Rejection of a Female Therapist'

I don't trust 'HER' .'SHE' failed me again. Until I learn to trust the feminine, I remain crippled.

'Death Wish'

They taught me to betray myself and I am sickened by all the pain, rage and shame. I feel despair and hopelessness. Would death be better?

'Fear Grows as my Defences Unravel'

The terror of feeling defences disintegrate and of confronting abject worthlessness, self-hatred and the evil, the pain, of that rejection.

Stage 8

'To Touch God'

My impatience to reach the goal of life, yet recognising it is by living the mundane reality authentically, trusting its value, we are able to grow and approach the goal more closely.

'Need'

I must learn to love that part of me that was / is rejected. Only then can I stop sabotaging myself and heal.

'The Goddess'

Access at last to the Goddess within where I had imprisoned her. Now I recognise and honour her and my initiation begins.

COMMENTARY

On the spiritual growth achieved by the poems in Cycle One

Knowing what each poem means in isolation gives no indication of the progress made. This only becomes apparent when the trajectory of the Whole Cycle of Poems is considered.

Let us start from the poems in Stages One and Two. These describe the fear, pain, misery, loneliness and despair which result from the lack of contact with my own soul. This is a very dark place indeed and the only time I ever considered suicide. Yet the suffering gradually motivated me to consider what I could do to avoid it. The poem 'Broken' suggests 'I look within myself' and heed the 'gentle warnings, the tender hints which tried to point the way'.

Thus the adages 'to know thyself' and 'the Kingdom of God is within you' begin to inform me of where I needed to look for guidance for the journey I am on.

Stage Two ends with two poems: 'The Courage to Respond' followed by 'Fear of Freedom'. This is a perfect example of the dialogue between poems, where a confrontation with what I need to do to escape an impasse is immediately followed by a poem expressing my fear of taking that step. Yet the price for not rallying my courage to respond is very high, the loss of freedom and individual identity.

By **Stage Three**, further progress is made in that I recognise I need to outgrow a childish need for dependence on others, plus an acknowledgment of the need to generate love within myself that I can then share. There is a sorting out of what is important and what is not. Love is now recognised as a central principle of life. I still find comfort in the illusion of 'homes', but they are alien to what I seek.

In **Stage Four,** love is again a central theme, but here different kinds of love are considered, not just the exclusive 'couple' kind promoted by our culture. In 'I Love the Night' there is a sense of getting closer to the spiritual experience of being part of 'The All', with its benign recognition and acceptance of what I am. The miraculous power of love to transform ends this stage.

Stage Five in any cycle is termed the 'Dark Night of the Soul', for the suffering experienced here relates to choices we have made. These choices are not always easy and the consequences need to be confronted and owned as in the poem 'Barren'. Yet here again I demonstrated the yes / no of indecision first noted in Stage Two, and in the following poem 'Sterile', I refuse to accept responsibility for my choice of not having children and decide to blame someone else. A strange choice, for my parents had three children!

This desire to escape responsibility for my actions and blame others had reached a crisis point, which is dramatically expressed in 'A Gift of Love'. The artwork 'Projection then Reflection' (which accompanies the poem) was made in 1978 and predates this poem by eight years. I was already aware then of the necessity of acknowledging the two sides of my psyche, the masculine ego and the feminine soul, but I was not prepared for the shattering revelation when the two actually confronted each other as expressed in the poem 'A Gift of Love'.

When the opposites make contact as they did here, the archetype of the Self is triggered. What is triggered is *completeness*, not *perfection*, and the inevitable consequence is a state of conflict.

I became aware of projecting my weaknesses and faults onto my partner and criticising him for them – a typical reaction of the Ego, but the increased awareness of what I was doing was a horrifying realisation, only possible because of the archetype of completion – the Self – had been evoked and I could perceive my behaviour in its completeness.

A nightmare, yet a profoundly significant spiritual milestone has been passed, for here the opposites, the unconscious psyche and the ego were in direct contact. The following extracts from Jung describe the situation:

'Only the **complete** *person knows how unbearable man is to himself, for he is in a state of wholeness that lacks perfection.*

To strive after perfection is not only legitimate but is inborn in man as a peculiarity which provides civilisation with one of its strongest roots.

The individual may strive after perfection, but must suffer from the opposite of his intentions for the sake of his completeness.

This situation creates the psychological precondition for the need for redemption.'
(From Jung, C. G. 1981 C.W. Vol 9, part II, pages 62-71.)

That this is a seminal moment in the spiritual journey is expressed by Edward E. Edinger as a 'breakthrough':

'...the ego-self axis suddenly breaks into conscious view...The ego becomes aware – experientially, of a transpersonal centre – to which the ego is subordinate.'
(Edinger, E. (1972) p. 69.

He follows this by a description by Carl Jung which I have paraphrased:

'When a summit of life is reached, when the bud unfolds and from the lesser the greater emerges...the greater figure...appears to the lesser personality with the force of a revelation.....the individual...will know that the long expected friend of his soul, the immortal one....has come to make his life flow into that greater life – a moment of deadliest peril.' Jung, C. G. (1959) C.W. 9, I, para 217.

The difficulty and distress with which I experienced this breakthrough stands testament to the potential danger of such a confrontation. Had my ego been unable to assimilate the shattering confrontation with the Self, I could easily have been overwhelmed by it and my ego consciousness itself be endangered.

The appearance of the Self here created a crisis, for its appearance in this one poem marked the beginning of the truly spiritual aspect of the transformational process and prefigured the much more intense invasion by the Shadow in Cycle Two. The battle between the Ego and the Shadow had to evolve into a relationship of co-operation and final merger before the Self could become manifested permanently.

However this was not a permanent state of affairs and the last poem of Stage Five returns to a personal unconscious expression in 'The Virgin'.

Stage Six is a turning away from the deep personal excavations of the psyche towards interpersonal relationships. 'How do you do it' celebrates the tough love of those who are dedicated to facilitating the healing of others by their compassionate revelations of the truth of the client's situation, which are necessary if the client is to move on. The 'Power of Love' reveals that it is through our own experience that we are able to help others.

Stage Seven involves confronting an archetype. In 'The Eye of the Demon Queen' the challenge is to recognise a superior power and dare to surrender to it. In 'Lilith' – one of the Guardians of the Threshold is encountered. I am protected from going into dangerous and forbidden territory and only once I have grown in spiritual stature, by confronting my personal monsters and demons, will I be ready to challenge the 'Demon Queen'.

The other three poems in Stage Seven all deal with the personal monsters and demons that I have to confront and assimilate before I can face the 'Demon Queen'. All of these I have generated myself through creating fear by accepting untruths from others. Each time I vanquish one by challenging it and proving it a lie, I get closer to the truth.

By **Stage Eight** it is clear that the direct experience with the Self in Stage Five has left its mark and I am now hungry for its presence as expressed in the poem 'To Touch God'. However, in 'Need' I recognise there is another monster to deal with – the belief that I am a reject and impossible to love. *It is clear that only I can provide the love that will vanquish this monster.*

In the last poem of Cycle One, 'The Goddess' I am at last able to perceive my soul which I had kept imprisoned. I am awakened to the new possibilities that awareness of her power offers me.

Chapter Two

Cycle Two: Confronting my Demons & Coming to Terms with my Shadow

PRELUDE TO CYCLE TWO

There is a Gap of seven years between the end of Cycle One and the beginning of Cycle Two. This prelude covers those events and experiences during that period which are of major significance to my ongoing spiritual journey, for they qualified the content of the poems in Cycle Two which are the harvest of those experiences.

The end of Cycle One marked another change in the direction of my life. The focus now was on acquiring those skills and personal development that would prepare me for working as a counsellor/ psychotherapist. Previous trainings I had undertaken plus a new one I was about to begin required on-going personal therapy on my part.

Using the Enterprise Allowance, I eventually set up a counselling practice, working in a local GP practice plus working with private clients. Although initially I felt inadequate and nervous, I quickly came to love the work and relaxed into it.

At the end of Cycle One, my poems indicated that I was well engaged with my inner world and this deep involvement with counselling in my professional life was very enriching. The client/ counsellor relationship is an intimate one and where long term work is undertaken, the I-Thou relationship, so espoused by Martin Buber and which requires engagement at a soul level, nurtures spiritual development in both parties. Whatever the issues being dealt with, such a connection inevitably facilitates the counselling relationship.

However, it is a one-way relationship in that it is the client's issues that are the focus of the work. The relationship is also restricted to the counselling venue and confidentiality is paramount. These limitations on the relationship presented no problems as I had learned to keep my own counsel as a child and respected that these were necessary in a counselling relationship.

As part of the requirement of my professional body I continued to have personal therapy myself. This ensured that any issues of my own that might be triggered through client work or anything I needed counselling for, were adequately catered for.

The most enriching and nurturing relationship I had during my counselling career came through the supervision which we were professionally required to have, to ensure we were working safely with our clients. I tested out several supervisors.

My third one was analytically trained and as I worked in a humanistic way, using person-centred skills and a whole range of eclectic skills I had developed through the various trainings I had undergone, she felt uncomfortable with the way I worked and we parted company.

I was then blessed to find a supervisor who also had a wide range of trainings similar to mine and with whom I felt free to discuss all the aspects of my work with clients, emotional, psychological and spiritual. She was a spiritually mature woman of around the same age as me and I retained her as my supervisor for the rest of my counselling career. This was not a collusive relationship for she was professional in the extreme and was quick to question any interventions I made during my client-work, in order to understand my thinking and motivations.

I found this relationship much more nurturing and enriching than those with my own counsellors, for it was a peer relationship, full of respect for the experience and trainings we had each undergone.

That she was a woman was a bonus for me as I had always hoped to meet a female in my life that I could unreservedly admire and respect on all levels, intellectually, psychologically and spiritually. This in itself was a healing experience for me and did much to counteract the negative attitude to being female, which had coloured so much of my life. I would have liked to remain friends with her after our professional relationship ended when I retired from client-work, but as with all professional relationships it is very rarely an option.

———————

There is one major issue I need to mention here as it triggered off a reaction in me that informed the poetry in Cycle Two.

Sixty-five years ago the attitude that women were third class citizens and were best suited to being housewives and mothers, was prevalent. My two older brothers took delight in making fun of me, ridiculing me and having little to do with me – I was just their 'kid sister'.

Twice my career was jeopardised by men in authority. One destroyed two years of my work – accidentally! On the second occasion I was failed an assessment by an external examiner – to the shock and outrage of my tutors – who did nothing about it! A third occasion was about to occur…

When I was Fifty-two, I attended University to do an MA in Counselling and Psychotherapy. By then I had worked professionally for six years. During the first year the two male tutors were presenting the model of counselling I was extremely familiar with. During one group session I pointed out that I felt they were misrepresenting the model by the way they led the group.

This was a fundamental issue and I felt it needed addressing if they were to present the model accurately. I could have been wrong – there could have been a perfectly reasonable explanation of why they were choosing to lead the group that way, all I needed was their justification for doing so.

The reaction from the tutors was outrageous. They angrily accused me of undermining their authority – of trying to get some of their power for myself! It was very embarrassing and I felt humiliated in front of the group. From then on, I was marked as a trouble maker. At the time I remained calm but on an inner level there were eruptions.

It was as if the many occasions when I had felt put down, obstructed, ridiculed, humiliated and bullied all came together and boiled over. For the first time a part of my soul exploded within me, a part that had always been repressed. This hitherto repressed part confronted me – demanding I take the opportunity to claim the potential power she was holding.

This was my Goddess in full flight and I felt overwhelmed by the sheer power of this part of my psyche. The poems in Cycle Two describe the process by which I came to acknowledge and co-operate with this hitherto unconscious aspect of myself and which had the potential to make me whole. My Ego, and my Unconscious learned to work together, slowly uniting to form my True Self.

Around this time I had participated in a full day of Trance Dancing. An amazing experience which I think may have predisposed my unconscious to break through to my Ego.

Another element that may have informed my unconscious that I was ready to take this next step, was the presence in my life of a strong and positive female role model, my professional supervisor.

POEMS SELECTED FOR CYCLE TWO

		Dates
Stage One: 5 poems	Lilith – my Buried Goddess	22.11.1998
	My Female Shadow	22.11.1998
	Potential Difference	26.11.1998
	My Crucifixion	26.11.1998
	My Alter Ego and I	27.11.1998
Stage Two: 3 poems	A Rage for Living	24.11.1998
	Initiation	21.12.1998
	Heartfelt	07.01.1999
Stage Three: 3 poems	Disengagement	22.11.1998
	Mourning the Lost Magic	26.11.1998
	Coming Home	19.12.1998
Stage Four: 3 poems	To Lilith	27.11.1998
	Chrysalis	27.12.1998
	Pregnant Virgin	05.01.1999
Stage Five: 4 poems	The Turning Point	27.12.1998
	Mother	30.12.1998
	My Inner Child	31.12.1998
	The Island	09.02.1999
Stage Six: 4 poems	Paradox	29.12.1998
	Breaking Free	31.12.1998
	Transform	04.01.1999
	Defences	23.06.1999
Stage Seven: 5 poems	The Mother Complex	29.12.1998
	Two Worlds	07.01.1999
	Premature	24.02.1999
	Goodbye Dear Friends	27.06.1999
	Diminished	08.07.1999
Stage Eight: 5 poems	Whole	11.03.1999
	Need Love vs. Gift Love	01.07.1999
	I'm Not Who I Thought	
	I was	07.07.1999
	Nowhere to Go	07.07.1999
	Potentiality	16.07.1999

Total: 32 poems

C2S1

LILITH – MY BURIED GODDESS

What happened?
How did his violent attack on me
Awaken this magnificence?
Uncoiling deep within my cells,
My soul, my brain?

What Alchemy?
What mystical alarm?
An evocation of a timeless power
Goddess or Witch, who knows?

Aah! Lilith! At last, we meet.
A name-sake. Hidden.
But discrete and powerful.
Biding your time
To strike, invite, beseech.

I come, with joy. I surrender
To this merciless, magnificent possession.

_____

An inner crucifixion,
But no Madonna this.
No ascetic transfiguration,
No pure or virginal queen,
But Power – Formidable – Supreme.
Of God? Of Lucifer?
Of Heaven? Or Hell?
Meaningless sounds
In this seamless unification.

22.11.1998

C2S1

MY FEMALE SHADOW

I know you are there,
You exploded within me.
A small but immense power
That's spread to permeate me.
Or, 'Who' has spread?
Not an 'it', but a being.

My soul-mate?
But not external, intrinsic to my world.
An inner presence so profound
That steals throughout my soul,
Seducing me.

So, I am in love?
With what? With whom?
So tempting to place you out there,
Impose your power on someone else
And fall for him.

But then I am enslaved
To him.
Seduced,
By him.
In love,
With him,
And yet the 'change' is here,
In me.

A magnificent enslaving,
That jolts me from complacency
And sleep.
Commands I wake and live and be
Within – without – my potency.
Or its, or his, who knows?
Who cares?

Commanded to live!
To reach, to stretch and strain.

To grasp the furthest star,
The hardest climb,
The toughest way,
The deepest love so far.

An impetus to grow.
An awesome irrefutable demand
To be, to live, to grow
Beyond my wildest dreams,
To freedom of my spirit/soul.

I come, oh yes, I come.
How else to live my life?
Except in joyous consummation
Our marriage to fulfil – complete.

Yet no male this.
No masculine domination,
But female, an archetypal siege.
Seizure of power **within** my soul.
That seduces the latency in me **to be.**
To swell, to break unreal
But massive limitations.

Delicious bondage to an inner power
Commanding, seducing, beckoning me
To embody her.
To be **that**, who **She is.**
To dare, to risk, to be.

22.11.1998

C2S1

POTENTIAL DIFFERENCE

The spark leapt – and caught.
It plunged **this** into life.
No prelude,
No gentle introduction,
No subtle invitation.

A massive shock created this
Unstable, naked polarity.

A power point of ineffable disquiet.
A trembling, rippling, excruciating pitch
Of power.

Evoking – No.
Requiring – No.
Exacting its opposite polarity.
Wrenching it forth, from
A blind/mute potentiality.

A massive tyrannical edict,
That dictates – you be too – you climb too.
You stretch yourself upon the wrack of super-being
And break yourself apart – to be fuller, more of you
To meet the more than I.

I did not ask for this.
I do not seek agreement, acceptance,
Or your approval.

You have a choice.
Respond and be transfigured.
A quantum leap – Can you make it?
Or else? This dies.

22.11.1998

C2S1

MY CRUCIFIXION

My original crucifixion.
Oh, I remember that.
I felt the split.
I felt two parts of me divide,
And Eve, I could allow,
But Lilith – Oh dear Lilith,
I did abandon you
And paid the price.

Too late to say I'm sorry.
I hurt myself so much
In order to survive.

Survive I did – just.
And now,
Lilith wakes,
And demands recognition.

26.11.1998

C2S1

MY ALTER EGO AND I

We became engaged,
A dragon and a toad,
Or demon goddess
And defective mortal.

Engaged we were in battle,
Two mutilated powers,
One bound in chains
The other lame and warped.

Who would have thought
We could redeem each other?
We found it very hard to meet
For we repelled each other.

We fought a battle for supremacy,
Unaware that one of us was growing,
Fuelled by stifled rage,
Augmented year by year,
Until at last she burst her chains,
And by design or mishap
Freed her long-time foe.

But now we **know**
How much we need each other.
We form a whole, we are complete
We are Camilla Leon.

How lonely we were apart,
Siamese twins – sisters,
Joined at the hip (where else)
But torn apart by ignorance.

27.11.1998

C2S2

A RAGE FOR LIVING

The shakes,
That's how I know you're here.
Delicious sense of naughtiness,
Mischief – not evil.
Why call it evil?

A need to be special, to be a star.
To shine and scintillate,
To fascinate and captivate.

I love you, and I am afraid of you.

You could push me just too far,
To teeter on the edge.
Sheer magic, of that instability.
A poising on the brink,
A tortured hunger,
Which seeks to draw
And hypnotise.
Engulf, consume,
Mercilessly.

A rage for living, that tears apart
The fragile veil of conformity.
A consummate hatred of the norm.
Extreme, unconstrained abandon.

I love you, and I am afraid of you.

Performer – exhibitionist
That's what you are.
Oh, how you love to show yourself,
To strut and preen before an audience

Reveal your hidden charms,
Uncensored, unrestrained.
Freedom personified,
Raw naked conflagration,
That burns so high and hot in you.

I love you, and I am afraid of you.

Your insistent invitation
To open up the door
To let you in, or out,
I don't know which,
But I fear your power,
Your colossal need
TO BE!

I fear I would be overwhelmed,
Drowned, burnt alive
In your too furious flame.

I love you, and I am afraid of you.

Frustrated exhibitionist,
Who tears at me,
And writhes around, inside of me.
Who bites and rips and tears apart my guts,
That's your expression!
To consume,
Yet never assuage your need.

Without you – I feel dead.
And with you?
Enthralling gleams of sensuality.
A gliding, slowly sliding
Womb of abandoned pleasures.

I love you, and I am afraid of you.

Too much, I feel you are.
Too much, I have been told.
And you screech with laughter,
To ridicule the timidity of men.
The fragile pathetic veils
Of this major sham,
Our refined and cultured sensibilities.

I love you, and I am afraid of you.

The way to madness,
That's what you are.
I dare not let you in
To flood me with
Abandoned sensuality.

Either/Or – so far,
To assimilate you into my world –
Not possible. My world would shatter
And I would die!
Or is this just me fear?
Could you, perhaps
Transfigure me
Without destroying me?

I love you, and I am afraid of you.

And so I let you seep into my veins,
Little by little,
And taste that sweetness.
By then – perhaps it is too late,
And I too, am lost in fascination.

I love you.

Sanity and madness.
The veil between
So perilously thin.
Eve on this side – Lilith on that.
I feel your heat, your power,
Your lust for life.

Can I contain you? Do I dare?
Or shall I just let go, succumb,
And let you live?

24.11.1998

C2S2

INITIATION

The fantasies have run their course.
Their power to enthral has waned.
Dreams no longer impassion me,
They have achieved their goal.

I am relieved:
This hot house fantasy is over.
An obsessive fascination –
Such exotic fluorescence
Could not survive,
Just exacerbated and inflamed my need.
Submerged in dreams,
I cast off into infinity.

Was that its purpose?
This colossal power, that shattered all pretences,
That honed in on just that inflamed need,
Where gentler, refined sensibilities,
Would have demurred to touch?
You blasted through all niceties
And dared me to deny the truth.

I had not known the truth.
At least, I had learned **not** to hear its voice.
I had denounced myself in favour of all others,
And hence the voice – was disconnected.

The confrontation – a nightmare unfolding,
For all denials came back to claim their dues.
A fight ensued, that escalated to a war.
A battle of extremes,
A monstrous, cannibalistic act.
Devoured and devourer would both be me.

Head on collision? No.
One side simply blocked the other,
And death ensued. An existential death.
A poisonous vacuum – created by my fear.

Yet, I simply floundered.
I did not know –
How to channel this massive energy!
I had to learn –
Step by step – by fantasy.

As if my guide – assumed the animus face,
And took me through the stages of initiation.
I was enthralled – could not – would not refuse,
And all my reservations, fears and narrow
Preconceptions, etherealized
In the monstrous scalding flame.
And truth – the existential, undeniable,
I recognised – could not avoid.
My blindness had been burnt away.

I was afraid – I tried so hard to refuse.
This did not fit – I could not see –
Could not control the sun,
And for my efforts –
I got burnt and scorched and flayed.

I tried to hold the ocean back and drowned.
My guide – he held my hand and dragged me down
Into the depths of madness.

I was mad,
To try and fight the Power of Life,
That had taken me. It had me by the throat,
And because I would not, could not, dared not be,
It shook me, beat me, drowned and shocked me,
Until – at last – I yielded.

Some-when, I took a risk,
Looked into my tormentor's eyes,
Only to see its pain,
I thought it was all mine.

I could choose not to fight.
I could choose to.......relate?

... Why had I fought?
What was the fear that shook me?
The power!

A rage for living,
That threatened my capacity to live.
I would erupt, turn inside out,
Passions exploding everywhere.
A hunger so immense – I knew it could not be filled.
I felt unequal – I felt diminished by the power.
It seemed to cauterise my veins – a power so fierce.
It stretched, empowered, challenged, forced me to grow.
Beyond my limit?

It felt so.
For I collapsed.
Burnt out – like death.
An energy – like the sun,
Had taken possession.

Do I torment you – my beloved guide?
I had not meant to hurt you.
I could not recognise your love for me.
I could not recognise the gift you had to offer.

And I have changed.
How could I not?
I'm slowly coming back to life,
With a difference.

For having been possessed
By such an awe-full power,
I have a hunger for it now.
And somewhere in me
Is the knowledge
Of how to attune to that elemental force.

Do I want it? Do I dare?

This time.......
It must be to align myself with it.
Another confrontation, I could not win.

Last time, she was merciful, reigned in her power.
Now she waits for me,
To signal my surrender to her power.
My allegiance to a greater wisdom,
Which I have to take on faith.

I invited the possession. I provoked it.
It possessed me – for a while,
And now, it waits.
Only a willing channel can serve its purpose now.

For, even as I write these words,
I can feel its power.
The Power of Life.

It is not 'I' that lives,
But life which shows itself through me,
If I let it.

To trust that much .... ?

To yield, surrender, acquiesce....?

21.12.1998

C2S2

HEART FELT

Having evoked it,
What do I do with it?
I want it to go away.
Perhaps this is partly why I smoked,
To deaden it, a smoke screen
To conceal, anaesthetise this feeling.

Here in my heart centre,
A burgeoning warmth, live and sensing.
A rippling current of joy,
That spills over to love and sensuous power,
That seeks ascension.

And next, my throat.
If that were freely open,
I feel that I would sing my joy, like a bird.
Feeling this – is that enough?
How do I handle this?
What do I do with this power?

An alien in my heart?

I love it and I hate it.
It is so close to me, within me.
Residing now – forever?
Here in me?
A beloved loving counterpart
I have to get to know.

No alien this,
Simply unrecognised – so strange.
Disowned it was and now reclaimed?

Magnificent possession.
I will yield – give me time.

7.01.1999

C2S3

DISENGAGEMENT

We think we have a choice,
To become engaged
With no awareness.

How can we little people know
With what we play and toy with?

To be engaged – truly,
To undertake a cosmic task,
Create a new beginning.

Two complementary potencies,
That spark, meet and create.

We did not have it, what it takes,
And so we disengage.
And yet, in truth, we never did engage.

22.11.1998

C2S3

MOURNING THE LOST MAGIC

Is it worth it?
Knowing more, I've lost the illusion.
Have I traded my passion
For cold-hearted awareness?
No, it's not the passion,
It's the beautiful illusion I traded in.

The magic of being in love.
The ecstasy and joy.
The delirium of being alive,
Of longing, fantasising.

For what?
The harsh knowledge
Of owning my own power.
To share with whom?

Full responsibility, that's what I've got,
To deal with all this rage and hate,
For all the times I have been hurt,
Betrayed, abused.

How to deal with this? I want to run away,
Transcend, avoid, be blind to it.
Yet Lilith has already whispered
Into Eve's ear, and she holds out the apple,
To tempt and bind the man
And he, in turn, blamed her.

Damn men.
Damn them for stealing power from me.
Damn them for forcing me to own it.
My power.

For I must use it to protect myself
And cease pretence of being only sweet and loving.

The rage in you,
The rage in me,
The rage in all the world,
Is just one rage,
Which burns time past, into eternity.

In hating you, it is the world I hate,
The sun, the birds, the flowers, sky and sea
And though this hate pours out to you,
It grows and grows, for you have set it free.

That used to be a love poem
And I cried to feel the other side,
Lilith's rage,
That she has been incarcerated with.

And every time I was put down,
And every time I was abused,
And every time, I was struck dumb.
Not so. I chose to hold my tongue.
Don't let them see they hurt me –
A pyrrhic victory that I'd won.

No wonder, so much rage.
A world of Eves – bereft of Lilith's power.
Sweet, loving, caring folk
Shat on each day by men,
Trained to be that way,
By women.

Us women have a lot to answer for.
Yet we have paid a heavy price.

I have been hurt.
Someone must pay –
So far it has been me.

Abused I was and now
I do that to myself
I don't allow my rage,
I hurt myself.

NO MORE!

Deep down inside, I cry.
For underneath this raging hate,
I dream of love.

I have traded
My beautiful illusion for truth
And I cry to see it die.

26.11.1998

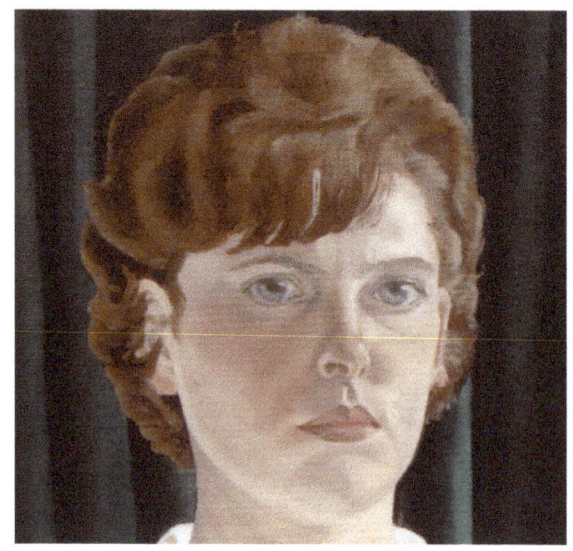

Eve

Eve Transfigured by Uniting with
Lilith

C2S3

COMING HOME

I let go of you and I came home.
That's how it feels.
I have withdrawn into myself,
I have decided to be real.

A deep sense of joy – of freedom,
I have at last broken free.
I don't need to live my life through you,
I need to live my life for me.

Compelled to put your will before mine,
To become an old woman before my time.
And now – I am free to love and be loved,
A need that is beautiful, a need that is mine.

19.12.1998

C2S4

TO LILITH

How hot you are my friend.
Can I, dare I call you that?
You have moved in,
We dwell together
And I can feel your heat
That percolates and energises,
Activating all of me
In different ways.

I feel your eyes look out of mine
And soften them with passions.
Not always fierce, but tender too
And I am left in awe.

I welcome you,
Please stay with me.
How radiant I feel
By you transfigured.

I marshalled Eve to keep you out.
I was afraid – I did not know
You could be good for me.
I feared your chthonic power.

And Eve is humanised by you.
Her spiritual zeal is softened
Leavened through sensuality,
Her dedication not so driven.

She loves you too,
Your surging power.
Between the two of you
An ecstasy is born
In which I too am bathed.

27.11.1998

C2S4

CHRYSALIS

From that space deep inside me,
A silence – so dense with need,
A break in the black continuum
A tendril of joy – seeks the light.

And she grows, slowly and uncertainly,
A new departure: A new attempt by
My soul sister, an alternative strategy
One that seeks to turn itself inside out.

To touch – so gently, but insistently,
The silent painful spaces inside.
To love them – oh so gently,
To cup them tenderly, with joy.

A reaching out that seeks to meet me,
Not to keep me out – but to touch me
And love me and meld with me, for
She longs to share with me
The love and joy she has inside.

Some-when, the fear transformed.
What else is there to fear, but alienation,
The last outpost of abandoned souls.

27.12.1998

C2S4

THE PREGNANT VIRGIN

I was asleep in my cocoon
Which I had woven assiduously
To keep me safe.
It was safe alright.
I was protected,
And that security became my prison.

My cocoon became a strait-jacket,
The limits being walls that kept me in.
And the cocoon crystallised and hardened
And it became my chrysalis,
Hard and unyielding.

And suddenly, I'm trapped. I feel it.
And this cocoon is now the edifice
Within which I break-down, break through
Transform and metamorphosis.

I cannot leave it yet,
I am still too enmeshed.
This strong container is still too strong
For me to break down, break through, escape.

Yet, now it is the means by which I'll grow.
Not yet can I dismantle this,
I need its womb-like safety,
To deconstruct myself and grow.

———————————

I do not have a choice.
Life is commanding me.
These fundamental massive changes
Are seed-like yet, fragile – precious,
And need my utmost care and nurturing.

But they *will* grow.
For this *is* the life that now takes hold of me.
I have no other life to live,

This *is* it.
And it *will* lead me,
What I must do, is nurture this.

I have no guarantees.
I do not know just what it is I'm harbouring.
I am the pregnant virgin,
I am the chrysalis.

And that within that now gestates,
I have on trust.
It is my privilege to manifest at length
Whatever progeny now grows.

I am the container and contained.
I am the chrysalis – I am the entity within
But *neither* do I own.
I claim no ownership of this creation.
Life has simply chosen me
To be the channel for this gift of life.

And so, I nurture it – with all my heart.
I trust – for what else can I do?
There is a power here
And I am awe-struck by its power.

I bow down in its presence.
I look no further for a God out there.
This power within demands my loyalty,
Obedience and reverence.

How else can I approach
This numinous chthonic majesty?
It is not I that lives
But life that lives itself through me.

It has me in its jaws
And like a dog that shakes the bone
Life shakes me hard
And will not let me go.
Life calls the tune.

And where I had refused to dance,
And where I had refused the invitation,
I'm being shown – I was not even asked.

Life *will* live itself through me.
I can refuse, resist, dig in my heels,
And simply – get broken.

The choice is mine.

I can rebel, refuse, not play the game.
I can refuse to live – and die.

Or I can open up myself,
Embrace this fearful power,
And put myself at life's behest.

I can retreat in fear,
I can withdraw from life,
Instead – this time – I will engage.

5.01.1999

C2S5

THE TURNING POINT

I imploded and imploded and imploded
Till there was nowhere else to go.
And when I'd reached that dead-end point,
I died.

I reached the place of maximum withdrawal.
No further place to hide, death is it.
And I curled up foetus-like in silence.

I rested unconscious, undesiring, at peace.
The world was dead to me.
Only deep inside myself,
A tiny pulse still flickered
And I slept.
So long I slept
In my cocoon.

And all these jagged, broken fragments,
That had torn my soul apart,
Dissolved in a sea of pain – that healed itself.
Just time and its strange alchemy.

Time and silence,
To soothe the splinters
Of too much longing.

27.12.1998

C2S5

MOTHER

She simply does not know
How to be honest.
I feel sick.

I'm so disgusted and outraged
By her manipulations,
Of which – I'm sure – she's unaware.

She pushes, pulls, coerces, bullies,
Anything to gain control.
Control me like a puppet,
And get the strokes / responses
That she needs.

Enough! – I will not do it.
I feel it all – so crystal clear
And most of all – I loathe her sympathy,
The most dishonest of all.

I'd rather have some honest rage
Than this power-hungry syrup.

Yet – I know my mother is a victim,
A victim of her complexes.
She is subject to them,
Therein lies her hypocrisy.

She will NOT BE HONEST!
She lives in her pretences.
She uses me!

Only if I let her.

30.12.1998

C2S5

MY INNER CHILD

My inner child has said:
"If you don't start to meet my needs,
I'm leaving, I won't play with you again."
And this time, I'm sure she means it.

So far, she has come out to play
When other people needed it.
"And what about me?" she says,
"What about when I want to play,
 Do you do anything about that?"

And I have to answer 'No!'

"Why not?" she screams,
And then begins to cry.
"Why don't you love me?"

And I am ashamed – for I chose
To side with my parents,
And ignore her loneliness.

31.12.1998

The Part I Mourned, Buried on the Island

C2S5

THE ISLAND

Deep within my soul there is an island,
Set in the midst of an ocean,
So far from the nearest mainland
It is forgotten – a deserted land,
Abandoned by humanity.

And on this island is a fortress,
With walls so thick not even the sound
Of crashing waves against the cliffs
Can penetrate – disturb the silence.

And in the basement of this fortress
Is the ruin of an ancient temple,
Hewn out of living rock
Deep in the heart of the island.

And in the gentle light
Which provides a soothing ambience,
An altar stands – at one end of the nave.
An altar – simply made, but beautiful,
Of marble or natural stone.

Upon this stands a casket,
Unadorned – white and virginal.
Within this precious box
There lies a part of me.

And it is this that mourns
And I too am in mourning.
I feel the grief, and that I share.
I long to open up this shrine,
Reclaim this part of me
And yet, I know I must not,
It is my sacrifice.

I have to walk away
And leave behind my heart,
My soul - for so it feels,
My inner child.

It is not time.
I have to leave it there.
I do not understand,
Perhaps I never will.
All I can do is hold in deepest reverence,
This part of me, this living sacrifice.

I have to walk away,
Yet I will share the grief.
I will mourn each day for you,
For that which was abandoned.

I love you – I would not leave you,
Yet life makes a huge demand on me,
And though I wish to stay,
Infuse myself into the casket,
To be with you, I must not.

For what lies here –
This living part of me,
Was violently torn out of me.

I did that – I had to.
The need in you – it was too great.
I had to exorcise your pain from me
And thus, I ripped you from my soul
And grieve you.

Each day I say a prayer for you,
And leave you in the tender loving care
Of those who comfort you.

For now – I grow,
And labour hard to protect you.
In time, I will reclaim you fully,
And then we will be free.

09.02.1999

C2S6

PARADOX

To be the devourer and devoured,
That I recognise – that does not feel safe.

Yet can one be container *and* contained?
It feels an 'ought', 'should', 'must'.
To rely on someone else to 'shore one up',
To lean on them for ....what?
Acceptance of my....? Experimental boundaries?
New ways of being – different strategies,
Feels not okay – risky? vulnerable?

It verges on that awful word – 'dependence'.
So how to be dependent – and yet okay?

Perhaps all I can do – is try it.

Perhaps, if I let go of controlling ALL of it,
Let them take some of the strain,
Could it be better?

Might they, in fact, emerge stronger
For the opportunity to support?
Support who? Themselves perhaps!

Have I in my too-conscientious operation
Infantalised them? Undermined their right to power?

It sounds an awful possibility
And I am so tired of it.

Right now, I need to just let go.
Rely on someone else to 'contain' me.
Who cares for the care-taker?

To be all for everyone –
The negative 'Mother Complex',
That founders on resentment in the end.

How *not* to do it?
It feels so alien.
Yet I need to,
That is becoming clear.
And who is there for me?

And this is where the paradox comes in,
For – I feel – it *should* be me.

I should be self-supporting.
I should be independent – strong.

So, how can I be both vulnerable,
And share my needs,
And still be strong and nurturing for others?

I'm lost.
Will someone else show me the way?

29.12.1998

C2S6

BREAKING FREE

"I love you so much,
I want you to be well again,"
My mother said.

Yet all she sees is that I am
No longer hers to feed upon.

I have let go.

I am no longer playing games with her.
She has to be her own reason for living,
She cannot live her life through me,
I will **NOT** have it.

I will no longer collude with her.
Her ravenous hunger,
To absorb me – live through me.

She hovers around me,
Follows me about.
She is like a hungry child,
Clinging at my hem
And I abhor it.

She does not love **ME**,
She needs an energy supply
To feed off.

How ugly that sounds,
How ugly it is.

I will live for myself and not for her.

31.12.1998

C2S6

TRANSFORM

Life has lived itself through me
In that set pattern for....oh!....so long,
And now it changes.
A different rhythm,
A different drum beat in my heart.

I cannot stop the change.
I can do nothing except submit,
Surrender, yield to it,
And I am afraid.

I do not know the moves, the patterns.
I do not know the steps to this new dance.
Yet life will teach me – if I let it.

"Do not resist", it says, "Do not fight me,
For you will change – you will transform,
Because it is the only life I give you."

What do I fear?
I fear I can't control my life.
It is not mine – my life lives me
And it will live me, as it sees fit.

I **must** let go.
This is the life that's given me to live.
Let go – have faith.
Trust life and love and being.

For life is pulling me away from here.
It's dragging me – resisting as I am,
Because I do not know the destination.

Perhaps there isn't one.
Perhaps the point is just......'let go'.

Stop trying to control the path I'm on.
Life knows far more than me,

I **must** yield to it, and trust
That what is right for me
Is also right for others.

I want to protect us all from pain,
Yet, they too have to bear
The consequences of the pasts
That they have freely chosen.

Oh God! help me to **be**,
To live the life I am.
Too long I have concealed myself.
No wonder life lost patience.

I have to jump,
Where else is there to go?
The path is there in front of me
No other paths are there to choose.

And yet, with all the fear and uncertainty,
My soul is peaceful,
For what is happening is real.
No pretence could feel so viciously.

In living life so vividly,
Some of it is hard to bear,
But it **is** real.
I could not falsify this anguish.

4.01.1999

C2S6

DEFENCES

It is not a safe place, this.
You invite me to expose my wounds,
To rip away protective scabs
That I have learned
Protect and start to heal me.

And upon your invitation,
I start to pick at them
And erode the safety they provide.

And what will happen then?
Will you be there to help me heal?
No – you will avert your gaze
From so much pain,
And leave me to my madness.

I do not blame you.
You think that what you do is good
And right, and will effect a healing.

But only if you are prepared
To love enough.
And that you will not, cannot do.

I show you the scabs,
The places where I hurt,
But not the wounds.
You laugh, and point in derision,
"But those are just defences,
Get rid of those" you say.

Of course, they are defences,
What else would you expect?

23.06.1999

C2S7

THE MOTHER COMPLEX

You are not "the complex" mother.
I see you now – dozing in your chair,
Very tired, withdrawing slowly from your life,
Faded, wrinkled – tired of living.
And my heart contracts with pain,
For both of us.
Where were you mother when I needed you?

How simple now, feeling tenderness for you.

Yet, you see, I know the other side of you,
And though I wish I could forget,
Indelibly imprinted on my brain,
Betrayals seeded by your own mother,
Seeded back to that Original One,
Where primordial unity was split in two,
And cataclysmic forces hurled apart,
The two anguished extremes.

Poles apart – of mother – Mother Nature
And the spirit realm – Our Father.

And thus it is our privilege,
To be the putty in the hands of these?
Humanity – the arena in which it is played out.
The majestic interplay of Yang and Yin.
Each pair of opposites,
Tremulously clinging and clawing away
From merging with its opposite
And neutrality – death to each extreme.

So each polarity must fight for its survival?
And spirit/matter; male/female;
Must struggle for ascendancy for power?

Is that the genesis of this mad world?
That the colossal, primordial 'Word' created?
That wrenched each pole from polar opposite

Creating duality out of silence?
So that these blind twitching nerves
Should spend eternity
Reasserting themselves,
By fighting to resist annihilation?

No mother – you are not the complex,
For I can see, you have stopped the war.
You gave up – when my father died,
For who then could you fight for power?

Yet, we can choose,
Not to identify with either side.
We can give fealty to monarchs in both camps:
Render unto Caesar that of mortal origin
And unto God, that belonging to the Spirit World.

And thus, we nullify the war.
We render each its' due.
We signal peace,
And from this simple choice,
A new era's born.

And the Kundalini spirit wakes.
And sensing the pregnant tension
Maintained between the two
With such a massive effort,
Rewards this evolutionary thrust,
Asserts ascendancy over both,
No longer either/or
By drawing them up into herself,
Back into an orgiastic ecstasy,
Pre-genesis fecundity,
Where all is possible.

A quantum leap achieved.

29.12.1998

C2S7

TWO WORLDS

I scramble back to this identity.
How hard this is.
I clawed my way back – heartbroken,
To leave my child behind.

I do not want to live like this,
Encased in an armour
Which enables me to survive
Out here – in this mundane world.

There are two halves of me
And one lives only underground.
Hidden, protected from the sun
Which is too harsh – and burns her.

And so, I surface,
Oh, so reluctantly!
And struggle awkwardly into my mask.
This capable organised being,
Who provides for the child underground.

My heart is there – my longing.
All that is meaningful.
For without this other world
How could that secret joy
Imbue this world with meaning?

I resented it, having to return.
There it was all mine – My World.
My Gods and Goddesses,
My Witches and my Demons,
Rich, with so much meaning.

I struggled back – resenting every step,
Hypnotically – magnetically seduced,
To stay there. I will return,
And yet right now – I cannot.

For to survive, for her my progeny to live,
I have to be in this cold world.
I have to earn a living, take my place,
Fulfil my role – do my bit,
In order that I can – occasionally,
Descend into my home again
And nurture my own soul.

These worlds – so far apart,
Yet each one needs the other.
Without this mundane world,
This other could not live.

Without the creative lustre
Of that – my other home,
This one would be pathetic,
An empty, joyless void.

And so I make the journeys,
Too and fro.
I guess I'm getting better
At changing gears.
I wish they were not *so* far apart.
I would like to mellow each with the other.

And each time that I make the jump
From here to there and back,
I think it is a little easier.

Yet – if I think to look,
It is there all the time,
My parallel universe,
The one so rich in love and meaning.

It's just – that I forget to look,
I forget my soul, my guide, my friend
Is right there, just beside me,
Waiting for me to turn and say 'hello'.

07.01.1999

'Psyche Awaiting Release'

C2S7

PREMATURE

I feel like a butterfly
That has emerged at last
Into the light of day,
Ready to fly and dance upon the wind,
Longing to soar towards the sun,
To play.

Yet I feel I am pinned
Right through my heart.
My wings struggle to beat
To counter this,
Which ties me, binds me down.

I stare – not understanding
This power that's holding me.

A shaft of light – arrow of steel
Straight through my soul,
My freedom,
My flight,
Delayed.

I wait – beaten – not broken.

Like the dove in its cage,
That hurls itself in maddened flight
Against the bars,
And mutilates and hurts itself.
An instinctual life/death fight
To realise its destiny,
Its intrinsic need to fly.

To flee away? escape?
Or advance towards?
Approach its nemesis or apogee?
Time will reveal.
Perhaps they are the same,
Two ends of one continuum.

And when the door is opened,
The cage's boundaries breached,
What then? Will she fly?
This blood bespattered dove,
Whose left wing sags.
Beaten, not broken
But battle-scarred.

Secure within its cage – the dove,
Secure inside its chrysalis – the butterfly,
And each will fight and struggle to emerge,
What then?

The damaged wing,
It just needs time to heal.
I stroke the head that droops,
I wipe away the drops of blood
Harsh against
The softly nestling feathers.

I gently lift and place you in my heart,
And warm you with my love.
Let my love surround
And cushion you –safe here inside.

The butterfly, held fast by fate,
Keep still dear heart, don't struggle.
It is no mortal wound that tethers you
It is enforced delay.

For when the time is right
The dove will heal and fly away.
The butterfly released,
Will seek to reach the sun
And joy will have its day.

24.02.1999

C2S7

GOODBYE DEAR FRIENDS

Too sad to express the feelings?
Almost.

Grief to let you go
Old friends of mine.
Mechanisms of defence,
Allies through the dark times,
Now no longer needed.

Yet you have served me well.
And though I must move on,
I thank you for your loyalty,
For you have saved my life.

My gratitude runs deep,
But life commands
A greater loyalty from me.

I hold you gently in my heart.
I will not abandon you,
You have been part of me
And shared my darkest hours.

I simply lay you down to rest
Amongst my saddest memories,
A bitter sweet resting place
Where you may sleep.

27.06.1999

C2S7

DIMINISHED

I feel diminished
For dear Lilith has departed.
Returned whence she came from.
I miss her so.

For 'tho her presence activated
Things in me hard to contain,
I felt so much alive.
I was augmented by her.
I felt a 'personal' being
And now she's gone,
I miss her.

Before I had not known her power,
Or if I ever did – so long ago,
That absence of her here
Felt normal,
And experienced as such.

But now I know.
My innocence of her is broken,
And I long to have her back again,
However much she dominates
My experience of living.

I feel depersonalised.
My sense of me – impoverished,
And 'tho I struggle hard
To compensate,
By channelling through other ways,
The magic gleam has gone,
And life feels bleak and barren.

I occupy myself, distract myself
With duty, obligations, what you will
And blank out the proximity of pain
With endless action.

But still I feel the vacuum left
By her absence.
She failed from lack of nurturing,
She needed love
And love she did not get.

She needed,
Oh, so much she needed
My acceptance, yet I had learnt
She was unacceptable.
I was afraid to love her,
And so it hurt to house her here.

Will she return – I do not know.
But now, you see
I *know* what I am missing.

It is the personal me that's gone,
And will alone, cannot sustain me.

08.07.1999

C2S8

WHOLE

That's how I feel.
Whole. Complete.
A centred strength.
No effort, no strain of trying.
A restful, but active space.

No fear, no pain,
But a deep-seated joy.
Serene power of authenticity,
Of true essential being,
Aligned to life.

I am complete.
I need no other to function well,
Though I love all I meet.
A simple state of being.
That **is.** That's all.

11.03.1999

C2S8

NEED LOVE VERSUS GIFT LOVE

Need love it was,
So painful.
So wracked with shame
And guilt and secrecy.

Left over longings
From the unloved child,
Infiltrating current love
And so despoiling,
Contaminating it
With pain and shame,
Humiliation too.

And all the fantasies
Tied up with it,
Those too corrupted
By a sick dynamic.

Only violence and force
Would – could
Defeat long-held denials
Of my need for love.

So, fantasies were violent,
Bereft of tenderness.
The love, more lust
Than mutual sharing of
A joyful hunger
That begged us to indulge it.

_____

And now?
A sweet relief.
A space of warmth.
A patient incubation
Of a passion, knowing it must wait.

For it is enough to love for now.
A love that blesses me.
A love that heals and sanctifies,
Embracing all my feelings.

A joy infusing me.
No urgency or need
To expend itself.
It is my life,
It is the quality
That blesses all my days.

This love has no particular focus,
But holds fast too
In its embrace
Awareness of a longing,
Much muted now
But ready to explode again
When it is appropriate.

For longing now
Is not a painful thing.
A playful spice
That flavours everything.
A sparkle in my eyes,
A hint of recklessness,
A gay abandon, kept in check.

This love – it is a gift,
Not just to me
For it exceeds my boundaries
And overflows and radiates,
Embracing all I see
Or hear or feel or know.

This love – synonymous with life,
Now healed and cleansed
Of all that poisoned it,
Arises fresh and uncontaminated
Born anew each day.
Exhaustless source of happiness and joy.

And if my love does not fulfil
The dreams that I had cherished,
It doesn't matter now,
For even that fulfilment,
And one that I still hold
With hope inside my heart,
Even that could not affect,
Detract or modify
This gentle loving calm
That lives within me.

1.07.1999

C2S8

I'M NOT WHO I THOUGHT I WAS

I am not who I thought I was.
What do I mean by that?
I feel different to myself,
My self-image has changed.

I like this 'me' so much more.
Gentler – more feminine,
More in touch with tenderness
And other feelings too,
As if I *can* now own them.
Before they didn't fit
The person that I thought I was.

I can respect my softness now.
Before I thought it was a sham,
An affectation donned for show,
But now I know it's real.

I can accept, embrace and love
The gentleness in me, the sensitivity.

Not now weakness to camouflage,
With hale and hearty bluff.
A quality, I coax and nurture it
For I can see its realness now.

It is authentic.
No feigned femininity,
But me, just as I am
And that I prize.

And all the other differences
That slowly infiltrate and change,
Mutate the being that I am.
As if the outer shell
Can now afford to pass away,
No longer needed to protect me.

For this new me, it is now new,
It is the one I was before,
Yet now, I do not need the shell,
I can accommodate
The knocks and blows.

I do not want to hide myself away.
It costs too much to conceal.
And if I do who knows me?
They know the shell, not me.

You see – I know that I am lonely.
Too long I have sequestered me
Behind tall walls, that fenced me in.
They kept me safe, but kept me lonely too.

For all the friends
Who would have really liked me,
They had no chance.
I was concealed, locked up
Imprisoned by my fears and safe,
But safe to mourn my loneliness.

For now – I need to love
And be beloved.
How else can I do that
But venture forth
From my self-imposed seclusion,
And take the risk
That even as I am,
I am enough.
I am loveable.

7.07.1999

C2S8

NOWHERE TO GO

Nowhere to go,
Nothing to aim for.
This present is perfect
For I am loved.

By whom? I don't know.
By what? Who cares.

My life is just so full of richness,
What more could I desire?
And should I die tonight,
It would not matter now,
For never ever
Could I possibly be
Happier than now.

No sense in this,
No outward change,
Yet something deep within
Has mellowed, ripened,
Come to fruition,
And life is sanctified,
And realised,
And justified.

7.07.1999

C2S8

POTENTIALITY

I'm not the person I thought I was.
I'm not 'what' I thought I was.
'Who' – 'what' – means nothing now.

A locus of evaluation,
A focal point of view,
An anchorage
For that fine spirit,
For life.

Two worlds that kept colliding:
The spirit world – transpersonal,
Esoteric and dispersed,
Against material and personal
The sexual and discrete.

Each side inhabited by turns,
Each world – a world apart
Separated by a chasm,
A borderland un-crossable,
Massively unyielding.

Confusion as I flashed between the two,
The worlds colliding.
Crashing soundlessly into dividing walls
That began to shatter,
And fragment.

The worlds started to infuse.
A madness – a kaleidoscope of
Incommensurables.
Invading and then infusing stealthily,
Creating yet another state
Partaking of the two.
An offspring – a merging of them both
To generate anew.

And as the fine dividing line dispersed,
So too the outer definition.
The life I was so sure was mine,
That sojourned here within me,
Does not.
Instead it is without, within
And everywhere.

It simply has an anchor point in me.
A point of view is what I am.
A junction box,
Connecting wildly different ways.

A fragment of a hologram
I embody everything.
By sensing deeply inside
I tune into it all.

The outer lines of me,
Do not be fooled.
That is not what or who I am,
It is just that life
Has found a foothold here.

And if I choose to loosen up,
Let go of non-existent
But imagined limitations,
I feel myself expand beyond,
Beyond myself.

For that is but a mirage
That fools me into diminishing
What I can be.

I have no right to do that.
My privilege – to be aware
Of life as it unfolds
Reveals itself majestically – mysteriously.

It creeps slowly on.
Not 'on' alone,

But 'out', 'above', 'below', 'behind'.
Beyond the limits of 'a' self.
Revealing life itself.

A freedom so immense
That there is nothing else,
Potentiality waiting to be fulfilled.

16.07.1999

CYCLE TWO

ANALYSIS OF POEMS & THEIR MEANINGS

Confronting my Demons - Coming to Terms with my Shadow

The poems were created from living the experiences. I could not always understand consciously what was happening as the experiences were so extreme and intense. I did write an interpretation of the poems at the time, but they were brief and inadequate and with hindsight and time to metabolise the events I can now present a fuller description of the meanings of the poems, for without some guidance they can seem dense and obscure because of their vivid expression.

Stage 1

'Lilith', 'My Female Shadow' and 'Potential Difference'

The three poems refer to the following event which was recorded in the Prelude. The public attack on me by a male tutor was an outrageous exhibition of bullying by a person in authority. This was the last straw for an aspect of my unconscious, no longer prepared to allow me to accept such patronising and bullying behaviour. An archetypal figure of immense power (the Shadow) erupted within me, no longer prepared to be repressed it broke through to my conscious ego.

When I was in a safe environment, the poem erupted. I was shocked, but recognised the legitimacy of her rage. Why should women be bullied in this way? I perceived her as my Shadow, Lilith, that I had repressed. She was offering to augment my power. I had to have courage to accept it – for I had to grow to be able to handle such power. The choice to accept or not was mine.

'My Crucifixion'

I remember quite clearly the occasion when – as a child – I had felt my consciousness split. I was deeply conflicted because my instinctual sexual behaviour was unacceptable to my religious upbringing. This division of my consciousness was something that happened to me (an experienced event) and relieved the anguish caused by the conflict. Thus an instinctual part of me was repressed.

'My Alter Ego and I'

The repressed Shadow had been growing, fuelled by the bullying I had experienced over the years. Bullying that had been sanctioned as socially acceptable behaviour by the superior male in our Patriarchal culture.

Her power was now so strong she would not remain repressed. My Ego (Eve) and Lilith (my Shadow) battled it out – until I recognised how much I needed and wanted the power Lilith was offering. Together we formed a '*whole*' being I called Camilla Leon, derived from chameleon. This lizard has the capacity to change colour and transform. I use it as a symbol signifying that we all have the potential to relate to our repressed aspect – the Shadow and it is imperative we do so or it will control the Ego, whether we are conscious of it or not.

Stage 2

'A Rage for Living', 'Initiation' and 'Heartfelt'

These three poems describe the struggle I had to open myself to the power of my Shadow. The fear I had of being overwhelmed – the fantasies about what it would mean – my terror of not being in control, of going mad.

Here the Ego is being invited to surrender to the Shadow. Eventually the Ego recognises the enormous gift being offered, but needs time to decide.

Stage 3

'Disengagement', 'Mourning the Lost Magic' and ' Coming Home'

These poems describe the period of indecision. The Ego (Eve) has asked for time to decide, which the Shadow (Lilith) has granted. The Ego loves and hates what is being offered. The Shadow anticipates taking possession, but wants the Ego to surrender willingly.

In these poems I consider the situation if I refuse her power and also recognise the legitimacy of Lilith's rage. Eve without Lilith's power is weak, disempowered by the values of the patriarchal society we live in.

Stage 4

'To Lilith', 'Chrysalis' and 'Pregnant Virgin'

It is fundamental to the success of this potential relationship between the Ego and the Shadow that the Ego is very strong, having developed through Cycle One. If Lilith over-powered Eve, that would be disastrous. They have agreed to work together.

Now the Ego and Shadow are co-operating, each is exerting its own influence and the Shadow cannot overwhelm the Ego. Through the act of acknowledging the Shadow, the Ego is now getting closer to their goal, that of creating the Self.

The importance of this developing relationship is emphasised by Jung.

'*Over and over again he emphasises that we all have a shadow, that everything substantial casts a shadow, that the Ego stand to the Shadow as light to shade*, that it is the shadow which makes us human.' *(My emphasis.)*
A critical dictionary of Jungian Analysis, p. 138

Thus, to be fully human we must know, acknowledge and work with the Shadow. In the Pregnant Virgin it is acknowledged that Life itself is now controlling the transformation.

Stage 5
'The Turning Point', 'Mother', 'My Inner Child' and 'The Island'
'The Turning Point'

These five poems describe the breakdown. I was not mad or insane but withdrew inside myself and remained in this unconscious space until life had worked its healing on me. Much later I was able to reflect on my previous life and identify where I had gone wrong, where I had betrayed myself, in my relationship with my own mother and My Inner Child –part of me that I had buried – on 'The Island'.

Stage 6

The Alchemical name for this stage is **fermentation** and that is a perfect description of the process going on here.
'Paradox' and 'Breaking Free'
These poems describe the confusion of struggling to establish new behaviours and identify authentic boundaries.
'Transform'
I acknowledge my fear of no longer being in control – for I am aware that the life given me to live is not mine to control. In order to

thrive, I must yield to life itself and despite the anguish and uncertainty, my soul is peaceful, for what is happening is **real**.

'Defences'

I'm communicating with an imaginal therapist, who represents all those people who will recommend behaviours that are not safe for me. I will release my defences when I am strong enough to do without them.

Stage 7

'The Mother Complex'

This is a stage where I am refining my assessments on how and why we behave as we do. This is a world of opposites and by learning to escape their control we can choose how and where we put our allegiance and power. We don't need to take sides but respect what is worthy of honour, wherever it is to be found, thus avoiding a conflict.

'Two Worlds'

Exemplifies the difficulty of doing this, but also the necessity of honouring both for the opposites need each other and we can choose when and how we acknowledge them.

'Premature'

An acknowledgment that it takes time to metamorphose and I need to accept the opportunity to heal wounds incurred in my desire and haste to reach the destination.

'Goodbye Dear Friends'

These are no longer needed and can be released. I express gratitude for their protection when I needed them.

'Diminished'

The pendulum swings back and reverting to my familiar ego-centred personality is painful and inadequate. Such swings are a periodic feature of the development that is ongoing and we can learn much from them.

Stage 8

'Whole'

This is a simple description of how it feels to be whole. Now that the Ego and Shadow have become reconciled and cooperate, the Self which is the centre of the Soul is manifest.

'Need Love vs. Gift Love'

This poem contrasts with another poem 'Gift Love not Need Love' in Cycle One. Need Love is contaminated by 'left over longings of the unloved child' for she learnt she was worthless and unlovable and hence it was shameful to want love.

Whereas Love that is unconditional heals and sanctifies. It is a gift freely given. It exceeds my boundaries, embracing everything. It is a feature of the state of being whole – without conflict. It is a quality of life itself when it is allowed to express itself fully.

'I'm not who I thought I was'

Now I can experience the sensitivity and beauty of the soul and all the changes that are infiltrating me from the unblemished source.

'Nowhere to go'

Now I have reached this point I can experience the love and deep happiness that requires nothing else to perfect it. The present state is perfect.

'Potentiality'

This is a beautiful summary of the journey I had to take to reach this point of absolute freedom. I no longer experience myself as a separate being, but as a means by which life expresses itself. I am life and there are no limits.

COMMENTARY

On the spiritual growth achieved by the poems in Cycle Two

Reminder: The Self is the goal of this part of the spiritual journey. It is the centre of the Soul. It remains unmanifested until the Ego and Soul have integrated although it may be triggered prematurely as in Stage Five in 'A Gift of Love'.

The Soul appears in different archetypal forms according to the level of spiritual maturity I have reached.

Recapitulation of its appearances in Cycle One Commentary

It appeared first in Stage Five in the poem 'A Gift of Love' as the adversary. The I-Self axis has been breached and I confront the reality of the superior entity (the Self) and am almost overcome by it. It is the presence of the Self that highlights the Ego's judgment of my partner and I am appalled, for I have projected my own failings onto him.

In Stage Seven in 'The Eye of the Demon Queen' I am challenged to recognise the superior power of the soul and surrender to it.

In 'Lilith' I am faced with a personal face of a Guardian of the Threshold. I still have personal monsters and demons to vanquish before I can cross over the threshold into the spiritual realm.

In Stage Eight in 'The Goddess' I at last come face to face with the Goddess, i.e. my own soul.

By Cycle Two I am working at a greater depth, with archetypal energies. Cycle Two records the process of consciously confronting the Psyche/Soul as Lilith and the transformation of the relationship between the Ego and the Psyche over time, until the relationship is firmly established and I experience what it is to be whole. The Self is then said to be Manifest.

We can see this transformation as it occurs step by step through the poems of Cycle Two:

'Lilith' is triggered by an external event – being attacked by a male tutor. She erupts – no longer prepared to suppress her power. At last I recognise she has something I need, although I'm not clear who or what she is.

'My Female Shadow': Confusion. What or who is the power that is pervading me, that is commanding me '**to break unreal but massive limitations**' in order to embody the Soul?

'Potential Difference': The Soul speaks directly to the Ego and offers it the opportunity '**to stretch yourself upon the rack of super-being …to meet the more than I**'. Acceptance will transfigure the Ego. The Ego has to choose.

'My Crucifixion': I remember when my Ego (as Eve) and Lilith (my Soul) split apart.

'My Alter Ego and I': Two mutilated powers – my buried Soul and my warped Ego. Ugly to each other. United they will form a whole, but this has yet to be achieved.

'A Rage for Living': The fear the Ego experiences of being overwhelmed by the power of the Soul.

'Initiation': A reprieve. I am allowed time to choose. Terrified of her power, I collapsed – '**burnt out – for an energy like the sun had**

taken possession'. No wonder I hesitate. Yet only if I am willing can I become a '**channel of life**'.

'Heartfelt': Extreme ambivalence towards this '**magnificent possession**'. A presence that is felt as both '**alien**' and '**beloved**'.

'Disengagement': The Ego is appalled at the '**cosmic task**' it is invited to undertake and pretends it can refuse, feeling inadequate to the task.

'Mourning the Lost Magic': Awareness of what such a refusal involves, the acceptance of an impoverished state, sanctioned by the patriarchal society, in which I feel a victim of male power. Do I intend to remain so?

'Coming Home': Releasing myself from subservience to the male. The male represents the Ego-consciousness and releasing it signals a readiness to accept the power of the Soul.

'To Lilith': I address Lilith – my Soul. We now abide together. Eve (Ego) and Lilith (Soul) are powerful and complement each other. The Self will be born of their union.

'Chrysalis': The Soul that was imprisoned in a shell, is now breaking out of her cell and gradually extends to fill and heal more of me.

'The Pregnant Virgin': My Ego, which I have developed to be strong and to act as my security, has become a prison, in which I am isolated. Within this safety I now transform as life determines. A Higher Power is now in control and I choose to surrender to its control.

'The Turning Point': This poem refers to the stage at which I collapsed from the shock of the confrontation with the Self. Its arrival was too much to bear and it took time to heal and recover.

'Mother': Another monster of my own creation that I have generated out of my fear of being inadequate. If I were more compassionate I would not resent her neediness.

'My Inner Child': The pain my soul has experienced from being abandoned.

'The Island': The hidden prison of my soul. We both suffer from our separation which I enforced because I could not bear her pain – the pain of feeling unloved. At present I protect her from the harshness and alienation of this world but as I grow in my capacity to surrender to the healing power of the spirit, she will become free.

'Paradox': The devourer is Ego asserting its control. The devoured is the imprisoned Soul. The confusion arises because Ego feels it needs to be in control yet at the same time recognises it wants to be sensitive and vulnerable. Only by uniting with the Soul can both needs be met and the Self become fully manifested.

'Breaking Free': I am not yet free of this monster I have created. This ravenous beast that seeks to feed off me is not my mother, but an old pattern of mine that hopes to gain love and acceptance if I 'please them'. This also applies to the fear of being rejected if I don't play society's games. Only when I learn to be authentic will I become free and release her from the resentment I have projected onto her, which has no doubt increased her need for love.

'Transform': I experience resistance to letting go of control although I know it is inevitable. I acknowledge the superior wisdom of the Self, yet fear the unknown. The undeniability of this situation causes anguish, yet the reality of it is like a bedrock I can trust.

'Defences': Defences can be abandoned only when they are no longer needed.

'The Mother Complex': This title is deceptive, for it is not about the mother complex, but about the split between the two worlds. The conscious – material – ego – male, versus the unconscious – spiritual – soul – female and the conflicts between the two as reflected in our world. Only when we integrate the two, the ego and the soul, do the conflicts cease and we become whole.

'Two Worlds': Until Ego and Soul integrate fully there are always opportunities to feel pain and alienation.

'Premature': We are given a life-time and purposes. Fulfilling our potential is an on-going quest. Impatience with our situation doesn't bring release any closer – just causes pain.

The artwork '**Psyche Awaiting Release**' on the facing page to this poem is one I made over forty years ago and predates this poem by 22 years. The butterflies emerging from the figure express my desire to escape my limitations and allow my spirit to fly free.

'Goodbye Dear Friends': Gratitude and a tender farewell to those defences which have saved my life and accompanied me through the dark times.

'Diminished': I have lost touch with my soul and feel diminished and depersonalised. I had learnt that Lilith was unacceptable and so was afraid to love her. I miss her.

'Whole': The experience when Ego and Soul are united. The Self is made manifest.

'Need Love vs. Gift Love': Need love is contaminated with left over longings from childhood. Gift love blesses, heals and sanctifies.

'I'm Not Who I Thought I was': I welcome the changes I experience in myself as I let go of the shell around my soul. It takes time to transform. I see what my defences have cost me and take the risk of shedding them.

'Nowhere to Go': Basking in the experience of being loved.

'Potentiality': A review of the process of uniting Ego and Soul, which leads to a release of the little self and opens the door to a freedom to be whatever life requires of me.

Chapter Three

Interim Poems Between Cycles Two & Three
PRELUDE

Before one can start Cycle Three, the psychological issues that were dealt with in Cycles One and Two have to be completed. It is for this reason that a few poems appeared, triggered by events during the thirteen-year period between cycles Two and Three.

Between 2004 and 2006 I undertook a three-year training with Roger Woolger in his Deep Memory Process (Past Life Therapy). The experiences I had during that time triggered deep-seated unconscious material that needed to be acknowledged, owned and healed.

These are an important collection of poems, signifying the last issues that required attention before I could move on. I have entitled this collection of six poems 'Last Confessions'.

––––––––––––

Three more poems arrived in 2009/10. The first one is called 'Regret' and I don't think I could have written this until after my mother had died. I have entitled these poems 'Requiem for a Passing Era'.

INTERIM POEMS BETWEEN CYCLES TWO AND THREE

'Last Confessions' written in 2006

	Date
The Struggle	21.08.2006
The Goddesses	23.08.2006
Misogyny	23.08.2006
Life's next Move	24.08.2006
Fear of my own Power	25.08.2006
Disempowerment at Birth	25.08.2006

Int.P, LC

THE STRUGGLE

Rotten to the core
The apple Eve offers,
And I feel the shame
Of that corrupted gift.

A shame that I keep hidden,
A shame I am ashamed of
And that too, I try to hide.

I am so sick of hiding,
The fear 'it' will be seen
And yet it governs me,
I know it.

The more I struggle to conceal,
Push down, ignore,
The more it is revealed.
It shouts aloud
In the silence of my denial.

In trepidation – I retrace my steps
To where the 'it' is buried.
In mourning I last left her.

An altar, simply made and beautiful,
Of marble, a natural stone.
Upon it stands a casket, unadorned,
White and virginal.
Within this precious box
There lies a part of me.
That is the 'it' I speak of.

And yet the 'it' is priceless
The heart and soul of me,
Buried alive – to keep it safe.
Blasphemy of the worst kind.

This sacred gift is God given.
It should be exercised.
It needs experience to grow
And be shared.
It is not mine alone,
A sacred trust
I am refusing.

What is its crime
I strive so hard to hide?

I did not want to come again,
To live another life on earth.
I fought so hard **not** to be born
And caused us both great pain.

And my reluctance to be here
Is part of why it's buried,
That bit I left behind.
I hoped to keep it safe that way.

Some-when – I must *choose*,
To be born here,
To fully incarnate,
Assume the sacred contract
I agreed to.

And so, I struggle.

21.08.2006

Int.P, LC

THE GODDESSES

Splintered fragments of the feminine
Great Mother Goddess,
Divided up to decimate your power,
And each one crippled
In its own minor realm.

Which ones am I hostess to?
And which ones deny?

There is a hatred in me
So deep – so caustic – so profound,
For this irredeemable damage
To the mother of us all.

Yet perhaps she is redeemed
If recognising what was done
We honour her.

Perhaps – in loving
All divisiveness goes?

Great Mother
Help me to love enough
That I heal.

23.08.2006

Int.P, LC

MISOGYNY

There is a price to being female.
I am ashamed – I do not want to pay,
Yet there is no escape. Avoiding it
Has caused me endless pain,
Greater than any fee exacted.

Born into a world
Where I was not welcome,
Or so it felt.
I was a girl
I could have been a leper.

Yet even now,
I do not know
Whether I arrived
Already burdened
With Misogyny.

In some past life
Did I misuse, abuse a woman,
Or many?

Did I arrive already full of shame?
For what I'd done before.

And now I feel the shame of women –
Countless women,
Humiliated, abused, degraded.

I'm sure I've done my share.

How to atone?
How to redeem
To resurrect the Goddess?

23.08.2006

Int.P, LC

LIFE'S NEXT MOVE

Slowly I step further and further back
And the realities begin to waver.

I act 'as if' things matter.
I apply myself assiduously to what I do,
And the only thing that motivates me
Is the sense that 'I am being what I am'.

What that *is* I don't profess to know.
It *really* doesn't matter what I call it,
But being true, aligned, in tune,
That does matter.

The bigger picture – isn't mine to see.

I trust there <u>is</u> a bigger picture.

Each time I trawl a little deeper,
Stretch out – extend myself,
And the disparate pieces acquired
Some now – some long ago – some yesterday,
Are echoing themes,
Implicating processes and plans
I did not know were there.

Now – I can begin to intuit
Life's next moves.
I'm sensing, feeling, smelling,
Apprehending something new.

A tuning into a vastly fecund
And underlying meaning,
Still in the becoming.

All this hurrying and scurrying
All this intense and dedicated focus
All of it – vexatious to the spirit.

And yet, where else –
How else could spirit learn
Except to pit itself against
Mundane reality?

Time and Space and Material Form,
The thrust blocks from which
Our spirits grow.

24.08.2006

Int.P, LC

FEAR OF MY OWN POWER

Lilith is stirring,
Her powerful muscles, flexing
And unwinding, ominously.

Like the coils of a huge python,
She is at last enraged enough
To raise her head and insidiously,
But irresistibly, be unstoppable.

She will rise up and vent her power.
She will assert the power too long denied.
Her rage is flickering into life,
The flickering of the python's tongue
That warns her enemies – keep back.

I will not spare you now.
Too long I have awaited your mercy.
Too long I have held back my power,
A power that I **will** now use.
Beware.

This serpent power **will** rise up,
It will engage.
Be careful. She is not sweet and loving,
She is too full of rage
And rightful fury
At your cruelty to her.

She has withheld her fury,
Afraid herself of so much power,
Yet goaded far beyond endurance
She **will** exact revenge.

25.08.2006

Int.P, LC

DISEMPOWERMENT AT BIRTH

I *really* fought **not** to be born.
I knew the struggle before me.
I clawed and clambered hard to stay inside,
Too soon I had to face the world out there.

I came – and as agreed – by me,
I suffered disempowerment.
Alienation so great
In an emotional desert
That made me crawl inside myself and hide.

I deformed myself.
I survived by denying my own survival.
I crawled so far inside myself
I was no longer here.

Just a flicker at the centre of my being
And I bided my time.

25.08.2006

'Requiem for a Passing Era' written in 2009/10

	Date
Regret	09.04.2009
Nostalgia	09.04.2009
A Deeper Rhythm	29.05.2010

Int.P, RPE

REGRET

Dear Mum,
I wish I could have shared my love with you.
Sweet tenderness, to heal the pain in you
That made you hard and cruel to me.
I didn't understand.

Why me? What had I done?
That seemed to fuel a bitterness,
A rage in you.

When all the men had gone, I was still there,
And yet, poor substitute.
It was not me you longed for, loved and missed.
I simply was the last one left
To share your anguished years.

I wish I could have loved you,
Reached out and touched your loneliness,
But I was never right.

I feel I was invisible to you.
It was not me you saw,
But some deep wound in you,
And it seemed I was the salt
That made the pain unbearable for you.

You could not / would not see me,
The pain of some deep unmet need
Precluded me.

My very femaleness
A cross I had to bear,
That's how it felt
The sin that I was guilty of.

You would not let me in.
You could not hold me tenderly
In mind, if not in arms.

My tears are not for me,
My tears are for the love refused
Not recognised or valued.

So, when you needed someone,
And I was all there was,
I could not love you then.
I'd learnt to steel myself
Against the hurt you could inflict.

You let me 'mother' you,
But then it was too late for you,
For mothering had become
Devalued currency.
The needs they should have met
Had long since ossified
In your abandoned child.

You let me do some things for you
But made it clear – or so I felt,
It cut no ice with you.

I was and always would be
The enemy to you,
An enemy you learned to tolerate,
That's all.

And later, when you did reach out to me
Aware, perhaps, that time was running out,
I could not then respond to you,
I had forgotten how.

Impossible to thaw
Decades of frozen wastelands.

9.04.2009

Int.P, RPE

NOSTALGIA

It seems to me
That pain and sadness
Are like a requiem.

A gentle farewell
To fading wounds,
A wistful mist
That slowly clears
As the sun rises on the morrow.

09.04.2009

Int.P, RPE

A DEEPER RHYTHM

There comes a point
Where you realise....
Know freedom.

You've done what was required of you,
There may be more,
But now...this present now
You're free.

Nothing less than stardust reality is worthy.
Nothing else can tempt you into false pursuits,
Only the experience of 'being' feels true,
Incontrovertible.

The rest – not worth a thought – much less an effort.

Only the cooling breeze, starlight and silence
Are truly family – bondsmen.
The rest, contingencies, distractions,
Arbitrary fallings of the dice.

No longer cues to further drama,
Just a backdrop,
A flimsy inconstant flow
Concealing, revealing nought
Except the rolling on of time
And freedom.

So what then does one do?

Listen for a deeper
More primordial sensing,
A deeper rhythm
Underlying appearances,
Like deep oceanic swells
Beneath the choppy waves

Tune into something new
But very very old.
A soothing alien familiarity.

29.05.2010

ANALYSIS OF INTERIM POEMS & THEIR MEANINGS

LAST CONFESSIONS

'The Struggle'

This is a very complex poem which I will try to unravel. The apple Eve offers is evil / corrupted because I rejected and abandoned the other half of her soul which I called Lilith. I buried her alive (see the poem The Island). We will come back to her.

I had assumed a sacred contract which I did not want to fulfil and to avoid having to do so I fought hard **not** to be born. (I learned this during work I did with the Deep Memory Process (also known as Past Life Therapy, during the three years I worked with Roger Woolger).

In spite of my resistance, I was born. As a result, I rejected a part of me. This was a part that I could not reconcile with the religious dogma I was brought up with, which regarded Lilith as evil. I repressed her.

However Lilith is an important part of my soul and I could not proceed with my spiritual journey without reclaiming her. The work I did in Cycle Two, of reconciling Lilith and Eve was a major and fundamental part of my journey.

'The Goddesses'

This poem acknowledges the way in which the socialisation of women fragments them into owning only those aspects that are esteemed or sanctioned by men in our Patriarchal culture. I acknowledge my despair at the damage done and request the help of the Great Mother in healing that which has wounded so many women and men, for we all have a shadow side that needs re-owning.

'Misogyny'

I wonder if I was born already despising women? Being born a woman I would now have to share in the burden of being putdown, diminished and scorned. This would make sense if I was, in fact, taking the consequences of actions in a previous incarnation, when as a man I had abused women.

Did I arrive already with a sense of shame for what I'd done in a previous life and so was now having to experience the shame of women who had been humiliated, abused and degraded? No wonder I was reluctant to be born.

It feels right that I should suffer this way. Is that one way I can atone for my previous mistakes and redeem the Goddess? I worked through some of this in Cycle Two and by reconciling Eve and Lilith I have healed at least some of the damage done.

'Life's Next Move'

Many of the personal dramas experienced seem to make sense in the bigger picture, where the disparate experiences seem to fulfil their function of enabling our spirits to learn and grow through them.

'Fear of my own Power'

A timely reminder that in order to defuse the rage Lilith felt at being repressed for so long, it had to be countered with a recognition of the justifiable nature of her rage. So, what can I or any of us do to change society to improve the conditions of women?

Lilith's rage represents the feeling of millions of women

world-wide. Actions need to be taken to facilitate equality between men and women which might relieve their need for revenge. Public condemnation and punishment of men who have misused their positions of power, authority or celebrity to abuse women is another necessary step.

It would seem that efforts are being made on both these fronts. Lilith's feelings are a sign of the times and the necessary steps to accelerate the evolution of society are gradually being taken.

'Disempowerment at Birth'

A sentiment that many women could identify with, simply because they were female. Personally, this was reflected in the fact that my mother wanted only sons.

REQUIEM FOR A PASSING ERA

'Regret'

This poem always makes me feel extremely sad. I know enough of my mother's life to know she inherited this hostility towards women from her own mother, who adored Mum's younger brother yet did not love Mum.

I have much to be grateful to her for. Not only did Mum give me life, she also saved my life when I was a baby and got pneumonia. Mum had to feed me every four hours with brandy and milk, which was difficult with two other babies under four years old, Dad away with the army, and the house and area being bombed.

We did not bond positively after my birth. The energy turned negative and for my whole life I could never touch my mother without feelings of revulsion. I think this aversion towards physical contact between us was mutual, for the only time I remember her cuddling me was when her mother died. I knew she was seeking comfort and yet I couldn't bear it and struggled to get off her lap. How sad.

I truly believe I chose her as my mother because she was able to consolidate the attitude in me which was the particular issue I had to deal with in this life – the inability to trust women and abandonment of my own capacity to identify with my feminine identity. This was represented by Lilith – the feminine aspect of my soul that I had split off and buried and would need to spend my life reclaiming in order to become whole, so, I thank Mum for that.

They say your worst enemies are in fact the most helpful in your spiritual journey, because of what you learn through them. I can see that is true with regard to my mother, although I would not call her my worst enemy, more a worthy adversary. It was her inability to love me that inspired years of therapy and training on my part in order to heal the damage done and which ultimately inspired me to become a psychotherapist. So, thank you for that Mum.

I sincerely hope her spirit is aware of the above and recognises that I love her and am truly grateful to her for playing such a difficult role in my life.

'Nostalgia'

This poem speaks for itself.

'A Deeper Rhythm'

This signals a closing down of the work done in Cycles One and Two. A period of rest is suggested and an acknowledgment that issues that previously engaged my attention have been laid to rest.

There is a presentiment that a new challenge is on its way, without any clearer idea of its content, except for the sense that it will require a commitment to a deeper level of reality.

Chapter Four

Cycle Three: Recognising the Ego & then Surrendering It

PRELUDE TO CYCLE THREE

There was a period of re-orientation during the thirteen-year Gap between the end of Cycle Two in 1999 and the beginning of Cycle Three in 2012.

I had a second hip replacement operation in November 2000, (the first one was in 1989) and recuperated with my mother. This meant that Terry and I spent Christmas 2000 and the millennium celebrations with Mum, culminating in a fabulous firework display in Broadstairs harbour. This was a precious experience as Mum died late in 2001. My surviving brother came back from Australia to help with the formalities.

There followed a hectic period, sorting out Mum's affairs, renovating the bungalow and selling it in 2003. As she lived a hundred miles away and I was continuing with my psychotherapy practice back home, it was a very busy time.

I completed all my professional trainings with a Certificate in Person-Centred Art Therapy and A Certificate in Supervision. I applied for professional accreditation in 2001 and this was later raised to Senior Accreditation in 2007.

———————————

From 2002, I super-saturated myself in a very wide range of spiritually oriented workshops, conferences and trainings which included:

- A residential in Glastonbury (a sort of spiritual home) in Numerology and Sacred Geometry.
- I trained as a spiritual healer. This I had to discontinue as each time I worked on a patient, I poured copious amounts of sweat, like a mini-monsoon, dripping all over the person. Not pleasant. I never discovered what this was about.
- I attended demonstrations on mediumship at various venues plus monthly meetings with a medium channelling Angels, Ascended Masters and Divine Messengers, providing information on the Nature of the Divine, the Gifts of Grace, Spiritual Growth and Higher levels of Consciousness.
- On-going workshops of a year each on Embracing the Goddess, Penetrating the Veil (between worlds), Soul Retrieval and Earth Magic. The last one entailed a visit to Avebury and a crop circle.
- I attended a Conference on Crop Circles in Glastonbury and subsequently Terry and I attended another one in Marlborough. We were taken on a tour of all the local crop circles.
- Between 2004 and 2006 I undertook a three-year training with Roger Woolger in the Deep Memory Process. This was his term for Past Life Therapy. This entailed residential courses in/near Devon.

––––––––––––

In 2009 I did a two-week residential training at the East Meon Centre for Sustainability for a certificate in Permaculture Design. I loved gardening and had had an allotment for years. My interests were widening out. Subsequently I invested in solar panels – a good clean source of renewable energy. These were very expensive and it was totally uncharacteristic of me to spend so lavishly. However, I did definitely feel prompted to invest in them, which was providential, for it has now provided me with an income which has augmented the old age pension, and without which I could not afford to remain in my home.

In 2011, I was diagnosed with rheumatoid arthritis and began to gradually run down my client-work. I was then Sixty-Five and could legitimately retire and become a genuine OAP. However, Cycle Three was about to kick-off.

POEMS SELECTED FOR CYCLE THREE

			Date:
Stage One:	5 poems	The Canvas of my Life	27.02.2012
		A Cipher?	27.02.2012
		A River never runs Straight	27.02.2012
		Trying to Meditate	28.02.2012
		Obedience	05.10.2012
Stage Two:	5 poems	So Close	05.04.2012
		Wholly Other	20.06.2012
		A Necessary Burden	18.11.2012
		Balance of Power	25.11.2012
		Getting Priorities Right	08.12.2012
Stage Three:	2 poems	Right Now	20.10.2012
		Life Unfurls	20.10.2012
Stage Four:	5 poems	A Door Opens	20.10.2012
		A New Venture	20.10.2012
		To Be like the Sun	19.11.2012
		Conduit	19.11.2012
		A Different Drumbeat	20.11.2012
Stage Five:	2 poems	The Torment of my Abandoned Child	21.03.2012
		I am Judas : She is Love	27.03.2012
Stage Six:	4 poems	Self-Defeating	03.02.2013
		Hiatus	27.02.2013
		Pyrrhic Victory	09.03.2013
		Repentance	08.04.2013
Stage Seven:	3 poems	Learning to 'be' in my Body	17.02.2013
		The Devil's Temptation	08.04.2013
		The Goddess Overshadowing Windwhistle	22.06.2013
Stage Eight:	5 poems	Windwhistle	02.06.2013
		Yearning for Release	08.06.2013
		Witnessing Creation in Action	02.07.2013
		Dark Night, Early Dawn, Rebirth.	08.05.2014
		Dancing in the Light	18.05.2014
Total:	31 poems		

C3S1

THE CANVAS OF MY LIFE

Resistance causes rage.
Deep hatred of constraints.
So, just let go of fighting them.

And see instead they are the banks
Within which my spirit flows.
Not to be fought and railed against,
But the very warp and weft
On which my spirit grows.

A painter needs a ground
On which to paint.
He stands back and sees the view,
Does not analyse the strands
That form the canvas.

Just so – we live our lives in freedom,
The choice of what we say and do
Is ours, upon this ground,
This warp and weft,
The canvas of our life.

27.02.2012

C3S1

A CIPHER?

I've seen myself as nothing,
A void where power should be.
Despised the uselessness
Of being me.

Yet, if I take another look,
The circumference I had
Identified as me,
I'd see another dimension.
The circle is just a momentary state.

For if I change my stance,
I see another dimension.
I see a cylinder, a channel
Through which life flows.

The onus on me is just to be,
And allow the meaning to grow.
For it is not I that lives,
But life that flows,
And generates its meaning.

27.02.2012

C3S1

A RIVER NEVER RUNS STRAIGHT

I baulk at what I see as enemies,
Delays, obstructions to my wish
To play and freely flow.

The river of my life feels stifled,
Blocked, damned up, frustrated,
And I want to stamp my feet and howl.

Yet, what river have I ever seen
That does not insinuate itself
Organically into the land?

Only man-made canals
Carve up the land,
Geometrically.

With great delight the river wanders,
Describing loops and bows and vagaries,
Creating muddy pools and swampy lands
And pastures on its way.

A delight to frogs and fish and birds,
And all these living things
That need the river's cargo.

The river does its thing – it flows
And dances with the land it meets.
It yields, advances, erodes and recedes,
And together the land and river
Create an organic reality
That is beautiful.

27.02.2012

C3S1

TRYING TO MEDITATE

Wobbling on the tip of a needle!

Listening for the tone
That's just right?
Responding to the drum
I can't quite hear.
Seeking for the thread
To grasp and pull on.
Groping blindly for an
Elusive point of light.

A fool's errand?
This questing for connection?
A blind faith, supreme hunger,
Deaf trying to hear.
A striving to respond
To a note I can't hear,
Yet *feel* is there.

Like a sea creature, stranded on land,
I'm straining to respond to stimuli
Just out of reach of where I am.

Blind faith – a clever term
Yet I turn towards **felt** light,
Obedient to a truth I **feel**

And so I continue to wobble
On the tip of the needle
And wait.

––––––––––––

I pause and look out of the window,
And see my garden, so coherently real.
The frogs reappearing in the pond,
Obedient to their cue – this time of year.

The crocuses already flowering,
The daffodils following too.
A reality so exact and organic.

I am trying to glimpse a reality
Using metaphors I can understand,
Whereas, in fact, the truth I am seeking
Isn't out there, it's in me.

I imagine a grand superstructure,
Coherent meanings and purpose so clear.
A fine web of connections,
Underlying and informing what's here.

Yet the language is different.
Finer sensibilities are needed.
It could take me several lifetimes
To tune in to that sound.

All this striving and struggle
Is ridiculous.
As if I am in control – Big Ego!
I should know this by now – just let go,
It's the striving that gets in the way.

28.02.2012

C3S1

OBEDIENCE

It's such a simple thing
Once you've cracked it.
Walking a fine line,
Yet it's an obvious one.

For once you have chosen,
And 'choosing' is the trick,
Once you've chosen to walk the fine line,
It's simple and easy.
For on either side of the line
There's trouble.

To wilfully do your own thing
In spite of knowing otherwise,
Evokes guilt and then remorse
And then the need to placate,
Fuelling an ugly rebellion
That turns back on itself.

Shame and guilt,
Remorse and rage
When all I need to do
Is follow the fine line.

05.10.2012

C3S2

SO CLOSE

I feel obsessed with my escape
From this cocoon.
I want to be free of it.
Yet its sticky cohesiveness
Embraces me.

The more I struggle to be free,
The more I'm aware of being stuck.

They say the fight for freedom
Strengthens the butterfly's wings.
Develops the very ability,
That enables it to fly free.

I can see the daylight around me,
I can feel the warmth of the sun,
The prospect of freedom excites me,
And so, I push on and on.

Now is not the time to give up
Nor the time to despair,
Just trust that life is supporting
This striving for freedom.

I will get there.

05.04.2012

C3S2

WHOLLY OTHER

How irksome,
These vestigial remnants of me.
Like the scabs or scars
Of old forgotten wounds
That insistently intrude their presence,
And impede the yearned for
Transformation.

I would love to be free of me.
The habits, addictions to
Familiar behaviours.
The fear of letting go completely.
I wish I could be free.

There is a fear.
Should I let go
How do I know
I would not just blink out,
And all that I have striven for
Be suddenly annulled?

Yet I feel this stage will come,
My sense of separation
Thins more each day.

The tattered mourning clothes,
The widow's weeds,
The rotting shreds of burial cloth,
The flakes of outgrown snakeskin,
All sloughed off.

Soon I pray,
I will be fully lost,
And dying to that dream of life
Be born into the wholly other.

It takes an act of will
To sever those last links.

It takes an act of faith
To step into the void.
It is an act of love
To trust the invitation.

20.06.2012

C3S2

A NECESSARY BURDEN

Being human,
There are times it disgusts me,
This load of petty, dirty stuff,
Like a cart of steaming, oozing dung
I drag behind me.

To be free
Of all that's personal.
The ultimate goal...to let it go,
This smashed dismembered skeleton,
Defunct, unlovely and corrupt.

Release the tethers,
Untie the bonds,
Let fly the awful stench
Of the unresolved,
The stained and tattered remnants
Of this redundant past.

It may be thus.....
And yet, it is the womb of spirit.
Out of this stinking rotten pile
Is born the phoenix of new life.

What greater miracle than this?

That from this devastation
Can arise the shimmering spirit.
Released...transparent realm of love and dreams,
Reformed as dew, to slake the thirst,
Ensure survival.....
Of nascent fantasies and
Newly opened eyes.

18.11.2012

C3S2

BALANCE OF POWER

A subtle change in the balance of power
That's what I sense, but do I fool myself?

It used to be occasionally
I'd have an intuition, or a hunch,
And sometimes I would act on it
Or ignore it as irrelevant.

I'd spot a coincidence,
But see it as a 'lucky chance'
Just the work of serendipity.

But now.....

I reflect on these events,
And see in their fortuitous effects,
Not the work of blind chance,
But the interventions of spirit,
Revealing its presence
In guiding my life.

25.11.2012

C3S2

GETTING PRIORITIES RIGHT

I sometimes feel abandoned by my muse.
It isn't true, she keeps knocking at my door.
A shy visitor, unsure of her welcome,
Yet eager to pursue a friendship
She believes is possible.

She's at the door now,
Holding a precious gift for me.
Gently knocking and hoping
I will welcome her with open arms,
And attend her fulsomely.

But ego jumps in and wrests control.
"Come back another time,
When I am not so busy."

I blush now at my rudeness,
My harsh rebuffing
Of her so gentle approach.

For her, now **is** the time.
She lives in this **now** moment
And if I want communion with her
I too must live **this** moment
And honour her arrival.

How can I be so stupid?
To ignore the gentle promptings
Of my spirit?

My ego dashes off,
Intent on 'making time'
And I am dragged along
Resisting in her wake.
She's so busy, doing all these things
Making time for 'writing'.

Fanatically she clears the decks,
Responsibilities, self-created and consuming,
Riding roughshod over inspiration,
Still waiting to be heard.

For I know she is there,
I even know the gift she is proffering me,
And I am arrogant enough
To think that she will leave the gift
For my acceptance, when I will.

Yet these gifts are so elusive,
Like delicate patterns of frost
They fade and are lost forever.

On occasions, when she has visited
There comes a time when she would leave,
Her airy presence, exhausted.
And I would try and make her stay,
Intoxicated by her presence.

I wanted another gift, so greedy to the core.
I'd reach out to her and try with fevered fingers
To wrest from her the gift not yet displayed,
And grasp the filmy robe she wears
To stop her leaving.

Another false move. I am rebuked
As she disappears before my gaze.

08.12.2012

C3S3

RIGHT NOW

Just stop, right now,
And close your eyes.
Be still and listen,
Feel the life pulsing through you.

Is this you, doing the pulsing,
The breathing in and out?

What's going on.....right now?
Inside the being called you?

20.10.2012

The Dalai Lama, when asked what surprised him most about humanity, answered: "Man. Because he sacrifices his health in order to make money. Then he sacrifices money to recuperate his health. And then he is so anxious about the future that he does not enjoy the present; the result being that he does not live in the present or the future; he lives as if he is never going to die, and then dies having never really lived."

C3S3

LIFE UNFURLS

A nothing…..begins to be something.
A deathly pall, awakened to potential
Implicit in its being.

Instant in time, when hyper-readiness
Is triggered and crystallisation begins.
In the super concentrated moment,
Pregnant with the future seeds
Of genesis.

That ever-present origin, that makes
A genesis of each and every moment.
Each passing second is pregnant with
The following moment's state.

And so, this life unfurls.
I am the agent, but not the cause.
Life lives itself through me.

The future unrolls, step by step.
Where it is going, I do not know,
Yet I am caught in fascination.

Like a snake wooed by the charmer's pipe,
I follow the bidding of life itself,
To see where it is going.

20.10.2012

C3S4

A DOOR OPENS

Joy and a deep sense of gratitude
As the door swings open on a new vista.
I could cry with relief.

A long and painful hiatus is coming to an end,
And my faith and trust........so sorely tested,
Is being validated in the extreme.

My life has felt obstructed
For ever..........so it seemed.
But now, a new phase, long in gestation.
New shoots of its promise
Just beginning to be seen.

Yet never could I have foreseen this.
A new direction has been clarified
And one I deeply treasure.

20.10.2012

C3S4

A NEW VENTURE

At what point did this sweet venture start?

Today I moved to actualise a dream,
Not one I consciously conceived
But one which birthed itself in me.

How strange that events move forward,
Emerging from a vague inexplicit urge
Seeded back in time, unconsciously.

And then today, I took a step
To actualise and set in motion
A process still unknown to me.
Yet pressing forward its need to manifest,
Obedient to its command.
I am subservient to its aim.

I simply took a step, in faith.
I've learnt to trust these inner promptings,
And so I took that step.
One step which seems the first along this path,
A path that leads somewhere,
I trust that life itself knows where.

At some point in time
A massive change occurred,
And something that was potential only,
Existing in an immaterial state,
Crossed that line.

What is that power, that implacable force,
The catalyst, prime mover of events?
That subtly programmes the transformation
From profoundly buried dreams,
To crystallise them slowly into solid form.

20.10.2012

C3S4

TO BE LIKE THE SUN

The sun.
Emanating power in all directions.
Enlivening, a massive effulgence,
Explosive power, bequeathed to all and sundry.
Detached, beneficent, this fuel of life,
A universal blessing, bestowed on everything.

So unlike the paranoid path we tread,
With the furtive, craven glance of convicted sinners.
We trudge the mono-directional way.
We walk the plank to certain death,
Our self-elected doom.

Enchained by the shame of crimes committed,
Of the mean and spiteful things we've done,
We drag along our fantasised failures,
Engendered by our self-absorbed pasts.

We clasp our self-elected punishments,
Tomorrow's martyrs' fare and self-inflicted woes,
Like self-righteous, puny magistrates.
And judge with false humility
And self-gratified pride,
Our own imagined transgressions,
And seek redemption that is not needed.

STOP NOW !
Release the past and future
We can live now,
Unfettered by remembered guilt.

Live like the sun....
Each second, newly born,
And putting forth ourselves
In magnificent out-reachings
Like shooting stars, we too engender beauty.

For life in its magnificence,
Is all of everything.
It does not judge, discriminate,
It experiences everything.
And gulps it down with exuberance.

Carrion or feast…it's all the same.
Food of experience, metabolised to power
And energised thus, all life moves on
And embraces us with joy and laughter.

19.11.2012

C3S4

A CONDUIT

Each end of the channel must be firmly fixed.
This earthly terminal must be solid,
Welded to the mundane life
To take the charge it will conduct.

The connection...to be sound
Is tried and tested many times,
For trust to be implicit and profound,
Which allows the charge to flow.

It is not mine to master, my role
Handmaiden to the task bestowed.
It is not mine, this work assigned,
The best I can do is just enough.

I trust that I've been tested thoroughly,
That life has thrown enough at me.
Has strained the chains to breaking point
And more...to see if they will hold.

Dig in my heels into this human space.
Grip on to daily rituals and menial tasks.
For these affirm my recognition of
The part I play...to earth the power.

It's not my role to question life,
But...simply open up...keep out of the way,
And let this vast magnificence...be manifest.

19.11.2012

C3S4

A DIFFERENT DRUMBEAT

I lean out of the window,
See the darkened garden,
Feel cold air on my face.
Hear the waterfall
Chattering and gurgling,
And mysterious ploppings
I don't hear in the day.

No rule or schedules to live by,
Just a trip on the magical carpet of life.
Like flowing with the river
Where it takes me.

Each day…a mystery that unfurls,
Every moment redolent with wholeness.

What a joy.
To be free
To ride on the back of a lifetime
As it unravels itself to me.

20.11.2012

C3S5

THE TORMENT OF MY ABANDONED CHILD

I am the wound.
I am the sickness.
I am the salt in my mother's wound,
And the everlasting guilt.

I am my Saviour's wounds
As he hung upon the cross.
I am the vinegar,
Which did not assuage his thirst.
I am the nails that pierced his flesh,
I am the spear that gashed his side,
I am the crown of thorns.

I am the crack in the cosmos
That lets the evil in.

21.03.2012

C3S5

I AM JUDAS : SHE IS LOVE

I trudge shamefully to Golgotha,
She was crucified because of me.
I go on to the cave where she was buried,
In despair at my treachery.

Then on to the island
Set far from the mainland,
To find the fortress erected thereon.
Make my way to the dungeon
Transformed to a temple,
For the duty it performs.

There on the altar is the casket
I abandoned, a life-time ago.
Holding the part of me I rejected.
For eons I know she has waited.
I'm afraid to approach her now.

So, I kneel before the casket
Where she has waited so long.
I feel shame and guilt so deeply,
Remorse at what I've done wrong.

I said I would come back for her,
That "some day I will return".
But why on earth would she believe me?
Her trust in me must have gone.

"Just know I love and care for you"
Said as I abandoned her to hell.
What a blasphemous lie, what a treachery,
Like a Judas kiss, instead of "goodbye".

How long she has waited,
How will she greet me?

27.03.2012

C3S6

SELF – DEFEATING

My stomach aches with striving
Trying hard to get this right,
For it has always been the way
I've done things.

Unless the way is very hard
Requiring dogged efforts,
Determination and commitment
To overcome all obstacles,
I feel I don't deserve to succeed.
Yet it's not really what I'm after.

Instead, I relish the pitiful cheers
Of coming last in the marathon.
How brave, what willpower
To overcome such obstacles,
And still to carry one.

How they love a loser
With whom they can identify,
Or pity and feel superior to.
How tedious it has become.

For now I know there's
A more authentic way.
I only need to stand aside.
Stop all this business
And simply trust the process,
Don't force the pace,
Allow it.

I've identified with Sisyphus
At the bottom of his mountain.
Back bent to shove his boulder
Up the steep ascent, knowing
It would simply roll down again.
Achieving acclaim for martyrdom
Was the only role I knew.

For saints strewn along the way,
Perhaps it was right for them to suffer.
But here I have a different challenge,
To stop this silly game.
To let my ego off the leash.
For trying is not needed here.

I feel the rage inside me,
My efforts are not valued?
I jump about in rage,
Frustrated that old patterns
Cannot work here.

For ego, that I thought was dead,
Smells fame in martyrdom.
Wants to frustrate the goal,
By insisting I do it her way.

It will not work.
The challenge facing me
Is to **surrender.**

Allow the child to wander free,
For in the wilds and windswept moors
She will find the treasure.

I need instead to feed the child
Who wants to play, not sit here
Pretending to do the work.
Her heart is cold today,
Let her play. She needs some fun
To spice her life, inspire her,
Release the tension
Of trying to get this right.

I am a hard taskmaster
All I do is mess things up.
Forgive myself again,
For allowing my zeal to

Trigger off old patterns of control,
That persecute and stifle
The very things I want to liberate.

For, if in doubt, I push,
If I'm not sure,
I assume I'm being lazy
Or can't be bothered,
And push more.

And yet this time feels different.
I know old habits are redundant
Worse than that – obstructive.

So, what now?

Is it really so difficult to listen?

No, it's trusting the voice that's hard.

The challenge now is just let go.
And yet I'm so obsessed with **trying.**

"Follow your excitement,
Listen to your body", so I say,
And yet I still keep on
Bulldozing over me.

Mandela said it perfectly.
It is not weakness, smallness
That I fear, but greatness.

I weep to find myself
Back here again,
Defeated by the habits
Of a lifetime.

Rebirth is needed
Into a different framework,
In which I truly yield

And let the power through.

Not freeze, contract and moan,
As I huddle contentedly
In familiar ways of being.

But I fear to lose myself!

If there is a mountain to climb
It won't be me that climbs it,
For there is only one mountain
I need to scale,
And that's inside my head.

03.02.2013

C3S6

HIATUS

Being captivated by the muse,
Or being driven by will power,
Both can be exhausting.

Sometimes I need to play.
Be in a neutral space and
Come back to the pendulum's mid-line,
Not driven, at peace.

The cycle will move on – and
Inspired by insights that arise,
Enthused to give them shape
The process *will* begin again.

But today!
I'm relieved to feel free
Of the obligation to fulfil some need,
Of the muse, or driven by
My own motivations.

Let go – relax – and just be.

Without the muse, without my goals,
My life would feel empty.
Yet there's joy in just 'being' too,
And in the hiatus between extremes
Is a place I can savour them both.

And it is there, in the silence
That the whispers begin.
A subtle change in the ether,
Seductive pull of emotions,
Something is beginning to build.

It's essential to pay attention,
Allow the feelings to grow.
Best done by glimpsing
From the corner of my eye
Rather than looking directly.

Gestation takes time,
Premature birth is dangerous,
One can abort so easily.

Take one's eye off the ball,
Focus instead on the seed
And allow it to grow,
For its message
Becomes amplified
In time.

27.02.2013

C3S6

PYRRHIC VICTORY

I wish I could always feel loving.
Sometimes – antipathy arises,
I don't know why. I examine it.

What is there in that person
That irritates me so much?

She seems positive and caring.
She's a woman. Is that enough
To trigger my feelings of resentment?

She acts as if she has authority
Over me. An assumption I'll fight.
It evokes my desire to puncture it,
To refute the flimsy power, she wields.

In sly and devious ways, I thwart her.
And this betrays the fear that I feel.
It's the arrogant assumption
Veiled with smiles, that I hate.

The petty rules she enforces,
I lie to evade them.
And in her failure
To enforce them,
I exult and
Feel triumph,
Tinged with
Shame.

She smiles, yet I'm sure that she knows
I've lied – Do I care? – Yes, I do.
For in that lies my squalid little triumph.

I've vanquished her power so easily,
Part of me delights in that.
I've challenged the petty power she wields,
And, bare faced liar that I am, I feel empowered.
For that one little moment.

But the sourness
Of that triumph,
Gets eroded
By shame.

For I've misused my own power.
A crime I've claimed is unforgiveable,
For in giving me the benefit of the doubt,
She used her power with care.

And I now feel crushed
And ridiculous,
As I recognise
My pettiness
And guilt.

I must apologise.
Own my own meanness.
Pay the dues that I owe.
If I refuse to own my own deception,
The charge of hypocrisy
Will plague me,
In my mind,
If not
In hers.

I honour her choice to accept
The little tawdry lie that I gave her.
She suspected, and I knew she did.
In that lies her superior stance.
She gave me the benefit of the doubt,
How shameful that I took advantage.

To own my own deception.
How small it makes me seem.
I accepted the rules, yet baulked
When these subsequently came into play.

Atonement? I'm not sure that I can.
The rules I accepted don't cover

Discharge of debt in arrears.
So how do I pay what I owe?

Caught in my web of deception.
I span a web, and now struggle vainly
To escape its sticky grasp.

Misuse of power I've claimed
To be one of the worst of crimes.
And yet out of the woodwork crawled
Part of me that played that game.
The very paltriness of the situation
Magnifies my shame.

The triviality of it all embarrasses me.
Had I faltered under matters of import,
I could have understood my transgression better.
To be indicted in such petty circumstances
Emphasises the smallness of me.

Yet what good would it do to confess
And confirm her suspicions of me?
It'd spread a contagion of mistrust.
Might it undermine her confidence
Her ability to trust – everyone,
Not just me?

I have to learn by this fiasco,
And if I do – then nothing has been wasted.
I must remember how disgusting it feels.
For the shame of my squalid behaviour
Is a punishment I'd sought to avoid.

09.03.2013

C3S6

REPENTANCE

Reviewing my life,
It's not a pretty sight.
For though I strained
To do the right thing,
Presented to the world
A facsimile of good,
It's counterpart remained
Within my soul, unheeded.

I tried so hard
To get it right,
But right by whom?

To integrate is hard.

To own, accept, embrace
My own rejected face,
And see how I have pasted it
Upon the world out there
And piously disowned it....

Is hard......requires
That difficult repentance.

08.04.2013

C3S7

LEARNING TO 'BE' IN MY BODY

From 'doing' to 'being' is such a radical step.
If we're open, it puts us in touch with our life,
But being open requires a body that is sensitive,
Not the numbed out conditioned carcass
We have learnt to ignore.

We have to 'awaken' our bodies,
Yet my ego is resistant, let sleeping dogs lie,
For if passions awaken, body hungers do too
And what a challenge they are to its despotic aim.

There is fear on both sides:
On one side – of losing control,
On the other – of being enslaved.

I let down my consciousness slowly,
Into territory that is my own body.
It's like an alien space to my ego
That sees an enemy to rule.

Like a rider approaching a spirited mount,
I intend to control it for my selfish aim
Impose **my** will, which is all I can see.
That the horse may object, is irrelevant to me.

How stupid I am.
I want a friend, not a downtrodden slave,
Why pit its strength against mine?

For a wild horse is a proud noble creature,
Resplendent in its power and grace.
Exulting in its God given freedom,
And quivering with joy
At the end of any race.

Yet with arrogance based on ignorance,
I see an animal I can use,
And convinced of my right to do so,
I forfeit its loyalty and trust.

I use it, control it, and thus break its spirit,
And end up with a pitiful nag.
And the harshness and brutality
I've displayed to this animal,
Precludes any easy restitution.

A change of heart is called for.
A willingness to concede
That this beast has rights too.

For it is not a beast – a dumb animal.
A miraculous creation, complete in itself,
That has no need or wish to be mastered,
Though a friend it could be
Shown love and respect.

A perfection I had not recognised,
With a wisdom exceeding my own.
Its wisdom is rooted in its instincts
That have evolved, over eons of time.

Each territory of this body of mine
I've tried to colonise by force.
Imposing my language and expectations
Presuming I'd be understood,
And resisted its indigenous wisdom,
Couched in feelings I didn't understand.

Only slowly has my arrogance given way,
To a recognition of the problem.
My body and I use different languages.
We struggle in mutual incomprehension,
Of these parallel but alternative lives.
A conscious mind and an unconscious body
That *could* augment and enrich each other.

So I'm learning to use simple images
Imbued with a willingness to co-operate,
To invite my body to relax and heal,
And my body responds with new feelings.

I'm learning to release my arrogance,
My need to control and subdue,
And to inhabit this beautiful country,
Allow it to permeate me.

With infinite patience and tolerance,
Body's indigenous wisdom has prevailed.
I'm invited to join in an exploration of being
Which negates any need to control.

17.02.2013

C3S7

THE DEVIL'S TEMPTATION

"What's the point?" he chides,
"All effort is a futile thing,
The fruits not worthy to be won."
And thus, he aims to fuel despair
And undermine our joy,
Our faith, our trust,
Our joyful aspirations.

So, we have a choice.
But who in their right mind
Would swap the joy and
Massive exhilaration,
The elusive sparkle
Of exploration and play?
The pleasure of achievement?
For what?
Despair and boredom?

So, a challenge once met
May lose its charm, so what!
It bequeathed a joy
And celebration.

We could renounce its value
And get depressed,
Decide it was a futile goal,
Undermine its value.
But why? What for?

Each new project or quest,
Growth in its latest guise,
And growth, it is essential.
We either grow or wither.

08.04.2013

C3S7

THE GODDESS OVERSHADOWING WINDWHISTLE

Yesterday I left, a day early.
Unable to sustain an intensity of being,
Essential, unavoidable, in her presence.

An honesty, authenticity of being,
That allowed no place to hide.
As if she recognised the soul of me,
And in order to remain with her
I had to '**be**' that soul.

I could not sustain
Such raw exposure of myself.

I thought I knew me,
But like a hermit-crab
I had adopted a shell,
I felt safe, protected in,
I felt at home there.

She sees past the mask
Engendered by efforts,
To restrict myself to quotidian life,
Where I am left in peace.

A counterfeit is what I feel,
In the presence of such Primeval Power.

Raw nature, red in tooth and claw,
Cannot help but expose the camouflage,
With which I have concealed myself.
Too fearful of my nakedness,
A confrontation with life itself.

Nomads, scratching for survival
Live authentically or die.
Whereas I have learned a myriad ways
To 'pass my time', 'distract myself'
Complacent in my cushioned life.

To live with her each day
Requires a fealty to being
I am struggling to attain.

Let go of control.
Trust that life itself
Will live through me
If I allow it.

Yet loyalty to such an aim
Necessitates that I let go,
Abandon self-deceptions
Of who or what I am.

That seems impossible
Terrifying to the child in me.

Allowing life to live through me
Requires an attentiveness,
Tuning into a different pulse,
A tuning out of old allegiances.

To earn the priceless gift on offer
Demands I relinquish others
I'd learnt to trust and hide behind.

So, am I ready to take that step?
Abandon habits, opt for authenticity?

SHE responded:

'Stop pretending. Live the life I give you.
Abandon hope all you who enter here,
For hope is predicated on a fear of living.

To those who live in trust, hope is redundant.'

22.06.2013

WINDWHISTLE

C3S8

WINDWHISTLE

A silent stillness, so dense and palpable,
Impregnating me with awe.
Inciting, inviting me to **'be'**
My heart and soul expand.

Like a cone from the Scots Pine
That explosively responds
To the warmth and
Magnificent sunlight,
My heart and soul similarly yield,
And yearn to live in worship
Of perfection, so close to sacred
In this place.

My soul keens with joy
An inexpressible kinship with life.

A sharp crack of release,
As tightly bound cones
Yield up their offspring
To seed another tree.

The sun clears the tree tops
And silence acknowledges the grace
Of warmth and light,
Bestowed so swiftly
As the sun appears.
A reverence accorded to this splendour.

How hard to be here, present
In the midst of perfection,
Real. Here. Now.

I want to fix it, hold it, own it.
Love it forever,
Embraced/enveloped
By my love,
As I am embraced by it.

Let go of imagined boundaries,
Be one with it.
That's all it needs
To realise this dream.

My heart responds,
My mind bears witness,
Pays homage to creation.

To be – it is enough
Encompassed by perfection.

To be in love with living.

02.06.2013

C3S8

YEARNING FOR RELEASE

The pregnancy of being.
My soul yearns for release,
To turn inside out
So I am free to merge with it,
The all-encompassing.

Its silence grips me
With wonder.

I witness it.

So, if I yielded,
Turned inside out,
Was flooded, overwhelmed,
Subsumed by it,
Then how would it be witnessed?

The privilege of being me,
Or you, or anyone,
Is that of being separate,
Just long enough,
To see and hear and reverence it.

And when it is too much,
I tire and cannot hold the awe,
Shrink back into my separate self,
Refreshed, inspired,
Full of love – for it.

18.06.2013

C3S8

WITNESSING CREATION IN ACTION

Like a glass of pure water
Set aside from the flow
All surrounding.

No traces of selfhood,
No impulse to action.
A state of suspension
In the maelstrom of living.

A stasis – pure witness,
Sublime contemplation,
And joy of release
From separation.

Embraced by a presence
To which I belong.
The Grace of perception,
Our 'raison d'etre'?

To witness and honour
In gratitude and love,
The beneficence
Which gifted me life.

And having been blessed
And enabled by spirit,
Supported by mentors
And guardians.

Guided on my way
By the lure of something
Seductive and inspiring,
A mystery
I never could name.

02.07.2013

C3S8

DARK NIGHT / EARLY DAWN / REBIRTH

You arrive at your destination
Led by the rules of your race,
Rules laid down by ancestors,
Evolved from their experience.

And when you get there,
Exhausted by the effort,
Feeling proud of the victory you've achieved,
And look around for the anticipated future,
There is nothing and no-one to see.

What was it you had expected?
A landscape you'd recognise as familiar?
Whereas, what you've achieved is exile,
With no landmarks to guide your next steps,
And no-one around who can help you,
Or so it seems, when you finally arrive.

What you need is the explorer's spirit,
One who's prepared to go it alone.
Thrown back on your deeper resources,
Trusting in the life that's your own,
Having faith that the power that spawned you,
Is still guiding you from within.

For should you arrive at the summit
Of the mountain you'd perceived as your goal,
New vistas of experience are opened,
Quite alien to the ones you had known.

A new way of being is required
To direct your next steps in this land.
A wisdom that is felt,
Revealed to your soul,
Bypassing the rational mind.

You cannot determine your passage,
Old faculties no longer compute.

What signposts there are, cannot be read,
Only sensed by the whole of your being.

Faculties that were nascent, are now needed,
Their emergence requires your attention.
Focus on the glimmerings of wisdom
That replace the misconceptions you had.
This new world requires a transformation,
Its rarefied air can imbue your essence
With sensitivities attuned to new frequencies.

This period can be hard and disillusioning,
Precisely the effect that's required,
For old experience and prior understandings
Are ineffective, inappropriate here.

You have to learn a new language,
Constellated from deep in your heart.
Vestigial remains of a long-forgotten code
Will revive, as necessity demands.

This mode of being is not new, just
Buried deep 'neath accumulations of time.
Civilisation's great bulk of achievements
Have brutalised the soul's sensitivity,
Which now has to be refined.

For what you have acquired
By ascending to the peak
Of the challenges your epoch has created,
Are the tools that enable further progress.
The mountain itself, like castles in the air,
Was a mirage that led your steps hither,
However worthy it may have seemed.

Acquired powers, emergent properties,
Of the struggles you engaged in
As you climbed to the top,
Are the tools and the language to live by.
For, now you are in exile from all that was familiar,
From the world of conceptions you had learned.

Different values, new priorities, new ways of perceiving
Render all your old learning redundant.

Experience alone will make you fluent
In how to negotiate this future.
No wonder it is called a rebirth.

There is no-one to ask here,
You are now your own authority,
Like a scout sent forth
To test the terrain.

What formerly you'd projected
As some power to obey,
Was unrealised potential,
Beckoning you forth,
To assuage your spiritual hunger.

It is now centred in your deepest within.

Trust is your greatest ally.
Have faith in the life that you are.
For now you are a denizen
Of this ocean, called life.

You are,
No longer,
Just a mortal.

_____

Here in this vaster reality,
Everything is your friend and compatriot.
It all depends on your attitude
How much help and nurturing you receive.
Continue to love, release it into life,
It'll attract whatever you need.

For life is like a womb
Of never-ending possibilities.
Whichever route you take
Will be blessed with success,

If you devote yourself to its evolving nature,
With love your over-riding motivation.

Love is the language here,
Nothing else is needed
To illumine the pathway ahead.
So become that love that you are,
And merge with the ground of all being.

You don't need to seek some grand goal,
Every second is charged with its own sweet need.
All you have to do to fulfil your life,
Is expend the love channeled through you.

Love is a powerhouse of unlimited potential.
One must learn to channel this safely,
And not get consumed
By this spiritual fire.

08.05.2014

C3S8

DANCING IN THE LIGHT

I am stricken, paralysed, consumed,
By a love that pervades me.
It emanates from where? From whom?
Joy that embraces everything I see.
Thank you, thank you, is all I can respond.
To the all that surrounds and includes me.

I am lost in this ocean of being.
A joy, a beauty and truth so extensive
That refutes any boundaries twixt it and me.
Nothing is required to complete this.

There is nothing I can do to justify this gift.
A gratitude so immense, it exceeds all expression.
My soul and spirit soar free,
Merging and dancing in the being all around,
An affirmation of the oneness of life.

To wake each day with this joy in my heart,
Transforms, invites and births a freedom,
Dissolving any sense of separation.
I am, we are, it is.
Embraced, interweaving, immersed in life,
That refutes any notion of limitation.

These words, little bubbles of joy,
Wishing to share this experience,
Right here, right now, awaiting,
A consummation of everything in love.

A joy that longs to be tested.
My trust and faith spilling forth,
Desire their reality be demonstrated.
For whom and why? No need.
Life and love and truth and joy,
All facets of this life we are being.

18.05.2014

CYCLE THREE

ANALYSIS OF POEMS & THEIR MEANINGS

Recognising the Ego and then Surrendering it

Stage 1

'The Canvas of my Life'

Egotistical frustration disappears when I transfer my centre of focus to the Self.

'A Cipher?'

My value and usefulness come from being a channel through which life flows and generates meaning. It is not about me.

'A River never runs Straight'

Frustration arises when I can't get my own way, but my life is not lived in isolation and what I have to learn comes from interacting with the world around me. That can be a source of great delight for it enriches my life and gives it value.

'Trying to Meditate'

In the mundane world there are clear ways to achieve goals, predictable schedules and events. Yet the inner world is not subject to my wilfulness or ambition to achieve. Trying hard is precisely what not to do. It's about letting go and allowing.

'Obedience'

It is perverse to go against what I know to be right, and simply causes problems. It is much simpler to obey.

Stage 2

'So Close'

My ego is ambitious and wants what it wants now. I need to let go, enjoy the journey and go with the flow of life, for then I will get there at just the right time.

'Wholly Other'

Awareness of my current unpreparedness for the goal is frustrating and uncomfortable, but these feelings can mobilise my drive to proceed, as long as I keep faith in the goal.

'A Necessary Burden'

From the devastation arises the shimmering spirit. Without compost nothing can grow. Without the burden of being human there would be nothing for the spirit to transform. It's precisely my unlovely and corrupt state that provides the reason for me to keep going.

'Balance of Power'

I'm becoming sensitive to the possibility that spirit is instrumental in guiding my life. I will pay attention to these occasions. It could be important for me to trust them.

'Getting Priorities Right'

I still haven't got my priorities right and that's because I overvalue what I want and don't value my muse enough. I treat her as if she's at my beck and call when it suits me. That is a monstrous mistake, for what she proffers is priceless and transient.

Stage 3

'Right Now'

I take myself and my experience for granted, yet it is all a mystery and if we choose to pay attention, we may apprehend something unexpected. I need to challenge my jaded assumptions.

'Life Unfurls'

I am the passenger of life not the pilot, so it is intriguing to see what's coming next.

Stage 4

'A Door Opens'

My patience is rewarded when a new direction in life is revealed.

'A New Venture'

The past, present and future all seem to be coming to fruition in a way I'd not foreseen. Trusting in life's process, I respond to an indefinable prompting to take a step forward into a potential that is just taking shape.

'To Be Like the Sun'

How mealy-mouthed and petty our self-evaluations are compared to the magnificent freedom and potential that is waiting to be tapped. The future awaits our decision as to whether to participate in its endless opportunities and leave the past behind. Who needs it?

'A Conduit'

There is a saying that 'God has no other hands than mine'. It seems appropriate here, for life cannot happen if we are not prepared to earth it in our daily life.

'A Different Drumbeat'

The joy of being a passenger, dependent on the vagaries of life to determine the adventure for today.

Stage 5

'The Torment of my Abandoned Child'

Deep suffering endured by the part of me I abandoned. She blamed herself for my treachery.

'I am Judas, She is Love'

My guilt at having abandoned a part of me. How can I ever atone? I have at last come to reclaim her, as I promised, but does she trust me? Can she forgive me?

Stage 6

'Self-Defeating'

I fear letting go of old habits that are obstructing me. Unless I have to struggle I don't feel I deserve to succeed, but the challenge for me now is to surrender – yield to life and let the power through. All my efforting is blocking the process, for my ego is trying to prove something and my ego is the one thing I need to let go of.

'Hiatus'

New projects begin in the quiet period between the excitement of creative ventures and those driven by will-power. Enjoy this break in activities for life is already preparing opportunities you may wish to take.

'Pyrrhic Victory'

It doesn't pay to cheat, for the momentary victory is soured by the knowledge I lied and committed what I feel is the unforgivable crime, of misusing my power.

'Repentance'

How often have I judged others for failings that are also mine. Owning all those parts of me I have rejected is hard, takes complete honesty, but it is better to do that than pretend the fault arises only in someone else and blame them.

Stage 7

'Learning to Be in my Body'

I take my body for granted and assume it is my right to ignore or abuse it, yet it is a miraculous creation deserving love and respect. I need to honour it, tune into it, learn its language and make it an ally, so we can explore each other's resources and share them. The conscious mind and the unconscious body need each other to function and become whole.

'The Devil's Temptation'

Apathy is destructive. It will suck out the joy and fulfilment that is potential in each venture if we allow it. Each new challenge offers opportunities for growth and once achieved we can move on to the next one. Together they provide variety and richness to our lives.

'The Goddess overshadowing Windwhistle'

Windwhistle – a spiritual home. Life itself, experienced as Goddess, inhabits this sacred place and to stay there requires an honesty, an authenticity that dares to be naked before her gaze. Maintaining that is challenging to my sense of self. I'm not used to shedding familiar distractions which preclude being fully present, and tuning in to what is new and alien in this place, allowing it to seep into me, helping me to grow spiritually and lose my fear of freedom.

Stage 8

'Windwhistle'

I'm overwhelmed with love and joy at being embraced by such a sacred place.

'Yearning for Release'

Feeling separate is a privilege, for it enables me to witness and reverence the 'Whole' and be refreshed by it.

'Witnessing Creation in Action'

The experience of wholeness.

'Dark Night, Early Dawn, Rebirth'

An experience of awakening into a spiritual realm.

'Dancing in the Light'

Spiritual ecstasy.

CYCLE THREE COMMENTARY

These poems have a more transpersonal quality compared to those in Cycles One and Two. It is as if I step further back and can observe my struggles more objectively. By doing so I get a clearer sense of what I have to do in order to go with the flow of life and not try and control it. The poem 'Wholly Other' describes the challenges I face:

> *'It takes an act of Will*
> To sever those last links.
> It takes an act of faith
> To step into the void.
> It is an act of love
> To trust the invitation.'

It is these spiritual qualities I need to develop.

Although a temporary alliance has been established between my Ego and my Shadow, I experience certain conflicts and discomforts as I attempt to live my life in this new relationship. It is similar to the hard work that has to be put into any new committed relationship once the honeymoon period is over.

Each opposite will inevitably emphasise its own strengths. Learning to compromise, or better said, co-operate together to the advantage of both sides, takes time and a willingness to empathise with the other's point of view. With the Shadow there is the potential for archetypal contents to invade, such that possession and inflation can occur. With the Ego, there can be pride and hubris contaminating the relationship, if the Ego chooses to own for itself, new contents arising from the Shadow.

Stage One recounts the difficulties that have to be overcome and the discomfort these cause.

Stage Two is learning to let go of controlling things, to learn to flow with life and trust it will take me where it has need of me, takes time.

Stage Three is keeping faith with the goal is essential and it is rewarded when life unfurls in ways I had not expected. Life becomes an adventure into the unknown.

In **Stage Four** I begin to recognise that I have value as long as I am prepared to respond to what life requires of me. There is also a sense of joy experienced as a passenger awaiting the adventures life may bring.

Stage Five – as in every cycle this is called the **Dark Night of the Soul.**

The two poems here illustrate the **dangers of inflation**. In this situation there is an identification with the collective psyche, caused by an invasion of unconscious archetypal contents. Thus an archetypal content seizes hold of the psyche with a kind of primeval force and compels it to *transgress the bounds of humanity*. The consequence can be a feeling of immense power and uniqueness (hypomanic) or a sense of being utterly worthless and of no account (depression).

In 'The Torment of my abandoned Child' there is the reference to being '*the crack in the cosmos where the evil comes in*' a massively exaggerated sense of guilt, which unexpressed could lead to suicide.

In 'I am Judas, she is Love' the guilt, shame and remorse are levels of feelings which are vastly out of proportion to the initial behaviour which gave rise to them. It was an act of self-preservation, as a child, to block off feelings that were too painful to bear and it is inappropriate to now punish myself so viciously for an act of self-preservation.

Stage Five in any cycle provides a necessary safety-valve for the expression of dangerous levels of destructive energy.

It is worth noting that Inflation can have a positive – though still inhuman expression. The poem 'To Be Like the Sun' illustrates a desire that could definitely be called inflation.

In **Stage Six** there are many implicit commands that we learn as children such as:

> Try Hard
>
> Hurry Up
>
> Be Perfect
>
> Be Strong
>
> Please Others

These are not usually verbalised but somehow expected of us. The beauty of the goal to surrender our self-will includes all of these habits which will free us to respond to opportunities life offers us without these constraints.

It is not easy to divest ourselves of these habitual behaviours and in essence there is nothing wrong with them as long as they occur as incidental consequences of our living authentically, attuned to the Greater Will of Life.

The poems in Stage Six recognise the fear and resistance to changing what we know are self-defeating behaviours, but encourages us to do so.

By **Stage Seven** the poems suggest ways to increase our conscious awareness of ways to enrich our lives – through body consciousness, engaging in challenges and divesting ourselves of distractions that preclude us from being fully present to the life around us in the now moment.

In **Stage Eight**, there is a premonition of change coming, in response to the overwhelming awe and joy experienced in being alive, and the desire to meld with it. This premonition is realised when I experienced an awakening into a spiritual realm. The last poem describes my experience of spiritual ecstasy.

Chapter Five

What Happens Then? (After Cycle Three)

EXAMPLES OF CHALLENGES ON THE SPIRITUAL JOURNEY (C.S.J)

Towards the end of Cycle Three, I was granted an experience of becoming spiritually awakened and began the process of acclimatising to the many differences from the world I had been familiar with. This was followed by an episode of spiritual ecstasy.

These experiences were, I believe, granted in response to the deep yearning I had expressed in the poem 'Yearning for Release' and were a gift of grace, a powerful incentive to continue the spiritual journey.

However, such experiences can present hidden dangers which it is well to be aware of. To that end, I include a poem here to highlight such dangers.

TEMPTATION TO STRAY FROM REALITY

I may have sipped of the ecstasy
Characteristic of spiritual communion.
Recognised through that blissful joy,
 The ground of reality we seek.

Impatient to re-experience the ecstasy,
And looking to speed up the process,
A temptation to 'drop-out',
Seek redemption more quickly,
Find an easier route and a
Premature renunciation of the work,
Is a possible temptation at this stage.

Instead, this glimpse and foretaste of a future,
Can incentivise my willingness to struggle
With the frictions implicit in being mortal,
Intensifying my spiritual commitment.

For the joy and spiritual ecstasy
Experienced as a spiritual benediction,
Is characteristic of the distance travelled,
Reflecting the changing panoramas and
Prefiguring intimations of the stages ahead
Like flashes of light in the minerals on the path.

Seduced by these fascinating glimpses,
Mirages of a far-away destiny,
We may trip over some very present boulders,
We'd ignored as we 'tripped'
Into stages far ahead.

Come back to the present-day realities,
The true path we each must tread.
To the alchemical stages we still must traverse,
The events we are currently living,
And others we have yet to encounter.

10.04.2014

You could be forgiven for thinking that having completed Cycle Three, I had achieved spiritual awakening, but it is not a finite destination. Another term for the spiritual journey is the Evolution of Consciousness, which requires dedication and commitment and is an ongoing process, as is spiritual enlightenment.

The words sacrifice and sacred have a common root and to be ready to enter the sacred domain is a challenge and does require a sacrifice, although that is ultimately recognised as an illusion – the self-will of the Ego.

Let us imagine that you have completed Cycle Three and just stumbled over the threshold of the spiritual realm, thus gaining some insight into the vast new territory of the spiritual world *(see chapter 9 on the Urantia Book)* and the sort of challenges you might encounter.

———————

Let's take a quick look back at what has been achieved so far. I developed a strong ego during Cycle One by confronting my own demons and monsters, those things I created through fear, because of the mistaken beliefs I had been taught. By confronting and owning them, I vanquished their power. The strong ego I developed was essential before I could move to the next stage.

In Cycle Two I was confronted by the Guardian of the Threshold, in the form of my Shadow, which I took to be an enemy. We battled it out, until I recognised she was offering me a gift of power in Lilith, that augmented my own. Over time we grew to value each other and learned to co-operate. **It is their full integration that creates the True Self.**

The True Self is the centre of the Total Psyche as the Ego is the centre of consciousness. Until the Ego has fully surrendered its will there are still opportunities for error and back-sliding, and the Self is not fully manifested.

The Self/Soul is personal and unique. The challenge of the spiritual journey is to transcend the Self by refining it so that it can return to the Source. So, the Self/Soul one has worked so hard to create now has to be refined. How does one do that? Little by little. The Ego part of the unmanifested Self is perhaps the first challenge.

1. Being in control of our own life has seemed fundamental, even essential and the ego will fight its own demise.
2. Resistances crawl out of the woodwork, unsuspected until challenged. (Poem Willingly Accepting the Bridle relates to 1 and 2.)
3. *If I lose my ego what's left?* is a fear that arises. What can I possibly do without it? There is a fear of personal annihilation.
4. This fear is negated as the ego learns it has an important function to perform, that of actualising the Greater Will. It is now an executor of the Will of God / the All / Life itself, whatever term you like to use. Without the Ego's participation, the Greater Will could not be performed. (God has no other hands than mine). (Poem 'The Ego's Fear'.)
5. The Personal Will has to change its allegiance away from 'me and mine' to incorporate the Will of the Whole, of Life itself. (Poem 'The Horse Whisperer'.)
6. This change of allegiance has already been achieved once before when the ego recognised it was only a part of the Manifest Self, and learned to co-operate with the Shadow. A further change in its allegiance is now required to put its will at the service of the Whole, of Life itself. (Poem 'Chastened Again'.)

Having crossed the threshold of the spiritual journey, trust is essential. In a sense Life now takes over, for spiritual help, guidance and love nurture the transiting soul. The companionship of your soul and inner guides becomes a reality.

The notion of losing one's sense of self gradually transforms into a real desire to be free of all that is felt to be limiting, simply as a result of being human.

None of this is easy, but grace, a term that includes all the spiritual support, guidance and interventions you need, strengthens the determination and courage necessary to continue. (Poem 'I Am Loved'.)

Someone told me recently that it is better to focus on the journey itself rather than on the final destination. Each part of the journey offers new adventures and realisations to be treasured. It is an adventure. (Poem 'An Adventure Unfurling'.)

To confirm that all the above has been learned by me through experience I have included a few poems that underline these realisations and included the title of the poem by the issue it addresses. (Poem 'The Last Task'.)

Poems describing some experiences during the Spiritual Journey

Title:	Date
Willingly Accepting the Bridle	29.10.2018
The Ego's Fear	06.11.2013
The Horse Whisperer	27.10.2018
Chastened Again	24.09.2013
I Am Loved	22.02.2014
An Adventure Unfurling	26.08.2017
The Last Task	25.08.2018

CSJ

WILLINGLY ACCEPTING THE BRIDLE

The stallion looks longingly at pastures new
Just over the fence from his paddock.
He knows every inch of his prison,
For now he sees it as that.

He sees his master travel out each day
And he longs to know where he is going.
He knows his master would willingly take him,
Riding his mount with pleasure.

Yet our stallion still hesitates,
Reluctant to concede.
Not yet willing to acquiesce to the bridle.
And remains hemmed in by his own refusal
To surrender his will to his master.

In frustration he turns away,
Gallops around his current estate,
Angry at his own hesitation,
Hungry to pass through this gate.

He knows he can trust his master,
Yet he's loathe to abandon his freedom
To choose his own fate.

Yet the whole time he obsesses
With the choice he has to make,
To yield his will to his master,
To willingly accept the bridle
Enabling them to act as one,
He is unable to move forward.

Stuck in his obstinate indecision
Enraged by his own frustration.

29.10.2018

CSJ

THE EGO'S FEAR

I am afraid. Of what?
If I let go,
Allow these thoughts to overwhelm me,
Pushing me to some abyss,
Where understanding seems pointless,
How am I better off?

What is there left to strive for
If 'being' is sufficient?
I want to put some brakes on,
Reflect and reach some conclusion.
Make sense of all this effort
The human race exhibits.

I want to stop this onward rush,
Take stock of where I'm going.
Yet life moves on, change happens
And I'm caught at some way station,
Fretting in the face
Of some grand mystery.

My little self – intimidated
By the implacableness of being.

Thus, the anxiety of the ego,
That fears its demotion by the Self,
Fears this presages its death.
That it will become redundant,
No longer have any power.

Yet, it **is** encompassed and valued
In its serving role.
For it implements down here
The meanings of the Self.

The ego is a priceless tool
As the executor of the greater Will.
Its role is one to be honoured.

Once this is recognised,
It becomes a willing ally.

Like a child relieved of fears
That had no substance,
Ego grasps its authentic role,
Of actualising
What the Self requires.

6.11.2013

C.S.J

THE HORSE WHISPERER

To wilfully choose
To cut off the branch
I'm standing on.
That's how it feels.

Yet I know I cannot proceed
Until I've made that choice.

To die before you die.
How simple it sounds,
How fearful to do.

Yet I'm tired of this stasis
This double bind I'm in,
Damned if I do,
Damned if I don't.
Is how it feels.

How patient is spirit
In allowing me to choose.
To bond with my master.
To prevaricate, hesitate,
Poised on the brink of what?
An abyss or freedom?

I need to listen to the spirit
The horse whisperer,
Gentling me. I know that feeling
From pony-trekking in my youth,
The love I felt for my pony.

Only spirit knows the true destination,
The route by which it is reached.
The stallion may rejoice in its freedom,
To charge off in all directions,
Exultant in its mastery of space,
Going where it chooses,
In love with experience,
Tossing his head with joy.

How patient is the owner
Rejoicing in the joy of his partner,
Enabling his physical perfection,
As he explores and exploits his potential
Running wild.

A wild animal cannot be forced
Or coerced into submission.
Of its own volition, the stallion must choose
To establish a connection over time.

And spirit waits,
Full of love for its mate.
A willing symbiosis is sought,
Not mastery, but unification through love.

27.10.2018

C.S.J.

CHASTENED AGAIN

These foothills hold a lot of dangers,
Misappropriation is one.
To appropriate to myself
What is not mine.
I need to honour the sacred.

If there is a role for me to play,
It's a privilege, a grace, not earned.
One cannot earn grace, it is bestowed
With love, and I am humbled.

I forget sometimes – still learning,
The 'I' that wants to take control
Has no place in this undertaking.
A sacred trust has been offered.

How dare I seek aggrandisement
When what is offered is a gift?
An opportunity to serve,
Not an occasion for me to shine.

I must be generous to my ego,
Be kind to the childish weakness.
To want recognition is understandable
So, I won't chastise or rebuke myself.

Just remember, remind myself again,
This ego has nothing to offer,
Except a willingness to serve.

24.09.2013

C.S.J

I AM LOVED

It's in the little things
I perceive spirit's care
And feel the arms of its presence,
Surrounding, embracing
And reassuring me.

Little things, obscure details
To others may seem trivial,
Convey interventions
In personal corners of my life,
Which reveal and demonstrate
A support for me personally.

This touches me deeply,
Inspires a humility,
That within this vast conurbation
I matter and am loved.

To perceive these acts of Grace
Requires attention to detail,
That can easily be obscured
In the noise of everyday life.

But it's just in the denseness of living
That spirit can best be observed.
Where the little interventions
Carry so much significance.
Nudging gently, yet insistently
My spirit awake, to remind me
That behind all appearances,
Lies the bedrock of a caring intelligence.

22.02.2014

C.S.J.

AN ADVENTURE UNFURLING

There is no me,
Just a point of view.
A locus of experience
That keeps flowing.

I'm an agent of life, and
Listen with heart and mind
For the promptings that tell me,
What's required of today.

How I love my inner family.
Beings I construct from reality?
Who invite and beckon me,
Surrounding me
With love and guidance.

Are they real, my beloved friends?
As real as I am, whatever that may be.
Ever watchful, they facilitate my life.

With joy and amazement
I experience their friendship.
Intrigued by their immanence,
And our joyful collaboration,
Realising the potential between us,
Pursuing the emerging pathway ahead.

What could I possibly fear?
When creations abundance
Is laid at my feet,
And the experience of each day
Is an adventure unfurling.

26.08.2017

C.S.J.

THE LAST TASK.

I want to be free of this identity.
It feels like I'm dragging
A chain-gang of prisoners
Reluctantly to their death.
Yet until we've achieved our purpose
I cannot let go of the gang.

We're all guilty by association
Also champions each one,
For we've all played our part
In the performance of this life,
And deserve the freedom to come.

I love you my strange bedfellows,
What a life we have lived.
Our aim, to find the road home,
Reveal the pathways we took,
Which may help others on this journey.

We continue this part of our quest.
Having crossed the last threshold
We bequeath our experience
With love.

The end is in sight,
Thank God, Thank Life
Thank you, Mother Earth
For the support you have provided.

25.08.2018

ANALYSIS OF THE MEANING OF THE POEMS SELECTED CONCERNING CHALLENGES OF THE SPIRITUAL JOURNEY

'Willingly accepting the Bridle'

The stallion here represents the ego that is resisting the challenge of accepting the bridle – as it signifies his loss of freedom to control his own life, despite the fact he longs to journey onward with the master he trusts. The master is the Self willing to guide the Ego to pastures new.

'The Ego's Fear'

Ego is afraid that he will die or become redundant if he acquiesces to the demands of the Self, until he realises he has an honoured and authentic role, to actualise what the Self requires.

'The Horse Whisperer'

The stallion, representing the ego, fears losing his freedom, although he recognises his master knows the route to the destination, whereas he does not. However, his master – the Self – allows the ego to choose, for he needs the willing co-operation of the ego, and is prepared to wait.

'Chastened Again'

The ego wants some recognition for its role, thus betraying its attachment to having power and being in control. Still learning to surrender to the superior will of the spirit, he acknowledges his error and recognises the privilege he has been offered, that of serving the spirit.

'I am Loved'

This poem speaks for itself.

'An adventure Unfurling'

Having surrendered her ego and become embraced by her spiritual family the transformed individual revels in the experience of being supported and guided by them, experiencing life as a glorious collaboration with them in which there is nothing to fear. An emerging pathway of adventures.

'The Last Task?'

Anticipating a sense of relief and fulfilment once the identified task has been completed, although with the recognition there may well be others.

Chapter Six

LEARNING THE HARD WAY

What Happens When Ego Interferes?

This situation occurred long after I had surrendered my will and my ego to the Greater Will – call it God if you prefer. This meant that I did not initiate projects or actions myself, but waited until I was cued into action by some external prompting – be it a need expressed by someone, or information received some other way. I had learnt from experience to 'trust the process of life' to organise things optimally and that surrendering my ego/little will was simply the recognition of that fact. The following is an example of my *failure* to live up to that and the consequences that followed.

Sometime after my partner, Terry, died, I realised I had some medical equipment that was no longer needed. This included a very expensive bed which had mechanisms to control various parts of the bed to assume the best orientations to potentiate the breathing and blood circulation etc. of the patient.

This is where my ego decided to get involved and thinking I was doing a 'good thing', I offered the equipment, including the bed, to the local hospice, so it could be used for some other needy person! The lorry came to pick it up, but the driver refused the mattress on hygiene grounds – fair enough – but took the rest away.

I knew I needed a bed for myself – my old one was creaking ominously, so I subsequently visited various charity shops looking for a base to fit Terry's beautifully sprung mattress that the driver had refused to take. I could not find one as the bed was of unusual proportions as it had been made to fit Terry who was quite tall. The last place I visited was the hospice warehouse where Terry's bed had been stored several days earlier, prior, I assumed, to being donated to someone.

They did not have a suitable bed base either. I drove away and just happened to glance in my wing mirror as I exited the site and was shocked and horrified to see Terry's bed, upended by the waste bins and getting saturated by the heavy rain. I immediately returned to the warehouse and asked them why Terry's medically designed bed was stuck outside with the rubbish getting soaked.

The assistant looked somewhat embarrassed when she acknowledged that 'it had been decided' to take out the motor and electrical components as being dangerous – and then throw the rest away!! I demanded that they bring it in out of the rain and return the bed base to me, which they did.

It was wet through and took a week before it dried out. I put it in the garage with doors open each end to form a wind tunnel, which worked well. The same driver came and helped me to get the bed base back upstairs to where it had been originally. At least I now had a bed base the right size to take the mattress.

A few weeks later, the company that had made the bed for Terry contacted me – a courtesy call to see if everything was working okay (I had not known about them). On learning that Terry had died, they said they would be happy to collect the bed and refurbish it for someone who could not afford the cost of a new one. I had to tell them what I had done and that the machinery side of the bed had been 'trashed' by the people at the Hospice warehouse. The man from the company was shocked and disappointed.

Had I not interfered, the bed in its fully working mode would have been refurbished by the company who had made it and offered to someone who needed one, but couldn't afford one.

That was exactly the outcome I had wanted and it would have come about had my ego not decided to take control and interfere with the smooth running of destiny/providence/life's plan. Yet again, I had to learn that 'Life' sees the bigger picture and by interfering I had obstructed the flow of life and forestalled the very outcome I had wanted. **This is learning the hard way.**

Chapter Seven

Miracles

Three Examples

Miracles are a proof of the interventions that Spirit can make in one's life in order to facilitate it. Nothing is likely to challenge people's preconceptions so powerfully as the experience of a miracle. To discount it as an 'Amazing Coincidence' is to miss one of the most profound incentives to question one's spiritual apathy and to challenge one's beliefs.

These can be so unbelievable that even when experiencing them, I have still been inclined to just accept them as providence / serendipity – because to look at them *full in the face* is quite shocking, even to someone like me who has faith in the spiritual world.

As I understand it, miracles occur when there is a very genuine need for them. I will give you a few examples from my own life.

1.   This happened when my partner Terry and I were on our world trip. He had converted his old van to carry all our camping gear and luggage. Dear old *Dougie* (the van) had carried us all over Europe and I hadn't given much thought as to how we'd deal with *Dougie* when we had to continue our travels by air. I'll copy the account from a record I wrote earlier.

'It occurred after we had crossed the Bosphorus bridge from Istanbul into the Asian side of Turkey. From there on, our travelling had to be by public transport or flights, so we had the problem of how to dispose of our beloved *Dougie*, the van that had been our travelling home for thousands of miles and we felt bad at leaving him behind. The options were limited to one. We could simply leave him at the airport, with permission from the authorities, but that felt like a total abandonment of responsibility as well as a shoddy way to treat *Dougie*.

'At the time we were in Bodrum, a popular Turkish seaside resort with a huge marina. As usual we were there 'out of season' and the place was virtually empty. We bought a hot drink and sat down outside a little café. The only other customers there were two people at a nearby table. One was a young western woman of around thirty, and the other a much older local man. Terry and I were still chewing over our options for *Dougie*, but at some point I started eavesdropping on the conversation that the couple on the next table were having.

The young lady was talking about her need to get hold of a car!!! We later learnt that she was English and was about to set up a restaurant in Bodrum but needed a form of transport to facilitate her plans.

I can't remember the steps we had to take to legally transfer the ownership of the vehicle to this young lady, but Terry and I were relieved to be able to entrust our beloved *Dougie* to a new owner.'

2.   I had driven Terry to his dental appointment. We noticed on the way that *Blue* (the car) was behaving oddly and we guessed we might have a flat tyre. We got to the carpark and I had barely opened the car door when I saw a young disabled man running (awkwardly) towards us. He shouted out 'You have a flat tyre' and

glancing down I could see he was right. 'Don't worry', he said 'I have a power pump in my car, it's for my wheelchair, but will easily inflate your tyre.'

Whereupon he inflated it for us, which gave us enough time for Terry to go to his dental appointment and then drive home before the tyre deflated again.

Miracles are often facilitated by 'strangers' who just happen to be on hand.

3.   This one was extremely significant to me and beggars belief that it could be anything but a loving intervention from spirit. I'll copy this from the Tribute to Terry I wrote and shared at his cremation service.

'When I was choosing the songs for the service, I became concerned that I hadn't told Terry enough how much I loved him and how important he was in my life and I felt deeply saddened I hadn't done more.

At the time I was looking for some small brown envelopes in which to put the photos that appear in the Order of Service. I'd used up my supply and went hunting for some more, first in the obvious places, then the less obvious places and finally in stupid places. I felt inspired to look in Terry's room.

He had a little wooden letter rack hidden at the back of a shelf. It was full of old pamphlets, used envelopes etc., and then at the back I found four of the envelopes I was looking for. I thanked my spirit family for their guidance, **but this was only the beginning.**

Back in my room I turned over the first envelope. On the front was Terry's name, written in my handwriting. Intrigued, I pulled out a letter I'd forgotten I had written, although I quickly recognised it. It was written six years before, in 2014, and begins:

"My Dearest Darling Terry,

It occurred to me that if I should die tonight, I would regret it terribly if I hadn't told you the following.

So I want you to know and, *I want to know that you know, that meeting you was the single most important event in my life and I love every bit of you."*

The rest of the letter tells Terry how his presence in my life and our relationship healed and transformed me. It gave me a sense of belonging that anchored me in this world and filled both our lives with meaning and love. The letter ends:

"With all the love I can possibly generate – plus some".'

How on earth could a letter I had written six years before and which I had forgotten, be presented to me in such a roundabout and bizarre way, at precisely the moment when I was anguishing over not having told Terry how much he meant to me!

It was as if Terry's spirit had lovingly intervened to remind me of this letter and what I had shared with him. If this isn't a miracle, then I don't know what is.

MIRACLES

Miracles abound.
They unfurl quietly.
You have to watch for them,
Observe their infiltration,
The shy intrusion of miracles.

Not in clouds of smoke
And loud acclaim they come,
But gently blossom,
Midst the noise and clatter
Of everyday affairs.
The bedrock of reality,
But, like the air around us
Can be taken for granted.

They are not less miraculous
Because we do not sense them.
It takes humility and faith
To perceive their presence.
The warp and weft of life,
Is so close, we overlook them.

So brutalised by the noise
Of our own activity,
We miss the translucent
Filaments of gold
That bind the seconds together.

Often in the detail
Of fortuitous events
We discount as coincidence.
Sudden 'unexpected help',
The 'lucky chance'.
We simply undervalue them,
Not open to the possibility
They were intended.

They need our close observance
And time to be reflected on.

For their 'unreasonable existence'
And hence their 'magic'
To be recognised.

We note the 'great disasters'
That clamour for attention,
But if we seek among the debris,
We may well find
In the heart of them,
Providence, Love, Fate,
Call it what you will, infiltrates,
And proffers opportunities
For needed transformations.

We tend to see what we expect,
And miracles are sadly
Misconstrued as luck,
Whereas the chaotic tumult
We accept as daily life,
Secretes them as its heart.

Take a risk, and just for fun
Assume a different attitude.
Pretend, just for a week,
That they are instead
'Intentional Interventions'.

Then the whole of life
Assumes implicit meaning,
That provokes in us
A startled apprehension
Of fragile insights
Into a deeper dimension.
That pulses with intentionality.
A living truth, that invites us
To participate, fulfil our role,
Facilitate a purpose we do not see
But which commands our reverence.

10.06.2012

Chapter Eight

Consciousness and the Mystery of Life

A MYSTERY

Consciousness looks out
And sees my hands,
And yet consciousness itself
I cannot see.

Mind bending on itself.
Without the me, what would it see?
But nothing.

The eyes that see, are mine.
The ears that hear,
The nose that smells,
The tongue that tastes,
The hands that do.

Without my agency,
And yours of course,
Mind would not have a purchase
On this thing called life.

There is a mystery here,
That life and consciousness and mind
Depend on me and you.

Regardless of the quality of life,
Rich or poor, clever or not,
We are the means
By which life lives
And consciousness gains meaning.

21.11.2012

Most of the time I took consciousness for granted, in the same way I took the air I breathed for granted and yet it is the ground of our being.

> '*We habitually focus on what we experience rather than <u>that we are experiencing.</u> But when we focus on the permanent presence that witnesses our ever-changing experience, we become conscious of consciousness.*'
> *Freke, F. and Gandy, P (2001) p. 74)*

I think the most powerful thing I learned relates to the mystery of life. I had experienced the 'Oneness of Being' which is accompanied by the recognition that my existence as a separate individual is an illusion, although I continue to **appear** to be separate individual, to myself and others, as I always have done. The following is a magnificent clarification of this:

> '*Enlightenment is the knowledge that all is One, but this does not mean we suddenly experience the world as an amorphous blob. Rather we understand that the essential Oneness necessarily expresses its infinite potential as the rich variety of life. Realising that we are not a person does not mean we suddenly become some sort of disembodied nobody. Rather, we exist on many levels:*
>
> *We are the Mystery, expressing itself as:*
>
> *Consciousness witnessing*
>
> *Psyche, within which*
>
> *We appear to be a person living a life in the world.*
>
> *Spiritual enlightenment means we discover that our essential identity is the Good. We won't need to* **become** *good. We will spontaneously act well as a natural expression of our being.*

We will no longer identify with the ego and so will be literally selfless.

We will know we are one with all that is, which is the experience of all-embracing love.

We will know that all that happens is the will of God, which is the experience of unconditional acceptance and unshakeable faith.

We will be intoxicated with the wonder at what has been staring us in the face the whole time, but which we have been too preoccupied to notice: <u>life is an awesome, incomprehensible miracle.</u>'

(Freke, G. and Gandy, P. (2001) p. 73)

The effort to consciously evolve, which is another way to describe the spiritual journey, leads to spiritual awakening and enlightenment. It was as if the spiritual lodestone, as I called it, created a magnetic pull on me – the spiritual homesickness I felt, and it was only by pursuing the search for its cause, that I achieved spiritual awakening and enlightenment, described by the above characteristics. I had finally come home.

Chapter Nine

The Urantia Book

At the beginning of Chapter Five I made reference to this book and "gaining insights into the vast new territory of the spiritual world".

When I was recommended *The Urantia Book*, decades ago, I found it an overwhelming book, for the territory it described was too vast and I couldn't find any way to relate to it, and therefore I put it aside.

Recently (2022) I picked it up – prompted by my Muse – and for the first time I could relate to a particular aspect of it. This is a major subject – the *"Thought Adjusters"*. On page 1191 of this vast tome of a book is written:

'*The Thought Adjusters' Mission:*

They have assumed the task of existing in your minds, there to receive the admonitions of the spiritual intelligences of the realms and then undertake to re-dictate or translate these spiritual messages to the material mind.'

It seemed to me that what I had termed my Muse, my Spiritual Guide had fulfilled this function in my own life. A confirmation that my Muse was not a figment of my imagination, but a divine entity on a mission.

There is another definition of Thought Adjusters:

'The Thought Adjusters are **powerful spiritual tools offered by "God" to us to connect with "His" force and wisdom.** With one of the highest universal technologies, they act as mediators in the internal dialogue, generated by each human being and the creative energy.'

De William S. Sadler has collated a lot of information from the book, which is available on-line, which includes the Origin, Nature, Mission and Assignment of these Adjusters – sometimes referred to as Mystery Monitors.

In retrospect, I can see how I have interpreted this spiritual entity within my mind according to the level of my own spiritual development. As a child of seven, I thought of her as a 'second mother– ' one who loved me and wished to comfort and support me. Later, I called her my Muse, because she communicated to me through poems. I tend to think of her as feminine, perhaps because that has always been the 'Holy Grail' for me, to find a female that I could trust absolutely.

She has assumed many roles so that I could confront unconscious aspects that I needed to face and integrate, *including* my Inner Child, the Goddess, my Adversary, Guardian of the Threshold, and finally, Lilith as the personification of the Soul I had abandoned and buried.

It was only much later that I became motivated to discover intellectually where the poems came from by exploring psychological literature and she (my Muse) received another name 'The Transcendent Function'.

Once Eve (Ego) and Lilith (Soul) created an alliance, they were on the way to create the Manifest Self, still in process. Yet that is not the end of the Thought Adjusters' role, for when I die (physically) we have the choice of moving on together as a unique being called the Morontia self.

The Thought Adjusters have the amazing capacity to shepherd our spiritual development along, without infringing on our free-will.

I recommend this book to anyone who wishes to penetrate the mysteries of the Spiritual World.

———————

As we are on the subject of books, the following are ones that I found inspiring. The first two are about remarkable experiences of individuals. The second two concern the afterlife. Details of all these are in the Reference section.

'Dying to be Me' by Anita Moorjani.

'Proof of Heaven' by Dr. Eben Alexander.

'Journey of Souls' by Michael Newton PhD.

'Destiny of Souls' also by Michael Newton PhD.

For those with a taste for exploration, I recommend the three books by Robert Monroe:

'Journeys Out of the Body', 'Far Journeys' and 'The Ultimate Journey'.

For sheer pleasure, I recommend: 'The Swan Thieves' by Elizabeth Kostova.

Chapter Ten

LAST WORDS

Coming to the end of this book has entailed lots of fiddly tasks to assemble the various aspects together. Feeling exhausted I decided to sit by our fish-pond, underneath the 'wiggly willow'. It was the first day for ages that the sun had appeared in a blue sky that had at last escaped from the heavy blanket of cloud.

I'd been there a while, when I noticed a squirrel wandering about the garden. She noticed me, but as I didn't move, she seemed unsure what I was and approached me with curiosity. Slowly, balancing on the rocks around the pond this beautiful little animal got closer until she was less than an arm's length away from me. She then sat down on her haunches and watched me with her beautiful black eyes. I sent love her way in waves of affection – and she stayed and stayed just gazing at me. I like to think we bonded.

At length she leapt into the fork of the tree just by my head to escape next door's black cat, who had decided to chase her. It is the first time in ages that one of the wildlife in our garden has got so close. It filled my heart with joy and the tiredness I'd been feeling disappeared.

You could say it was just chance, but it's the timing of these gems of experience that appear when I need some reassurance that I am loved and cared for.

Writing this book has been a labour of love. I have no idea if it will be of value to anyone, but having decided to write it, I felt I needed to do it as well as I could. I came across a section in a book called '*Serving the Task*' which I quote here:

"*When we speak of doing a job well, for its own sake, we refer to a shift in motivation in which we give the needs of the job precedence over our own wishes. We recognise that the proper accomplishment of the task may call for a certain amount and type of effort. For example, in writing this book, I may be aware that a certain passage isn't quite the way it should be; it is not complete, not finished. I can get by with it; it will do, but I feel that it is not the way it deserved to be and am pulled to meet its requirements, even if no one else notices the difference. The pull is not a compulsion but a recognition that the task is not complete **in its own terms**... the experience may be described as surrendering to the task, but it is a surrender in which the person is active and guided at the same time.*"
(*Deikman (1982) p. 112*)

I couldn't have put it better.

———————

And what about my 'Inner Child' that I had buried alive? She is now a very precious integral part of me. She is mischievous, and has a wonderful sense of humour, giggles a lot and pops up asking me to play with her if I get too 'intense'.

She reminds me of the little girl about whom I wrote a poem in January 2013 called '*Bubbles*'.

> I saw a young girl
> Blowing bubbles from a soap ring.
> She blew through the ring
> And watched in delight

The bubbles grow, then release,
Shimmering and wobbling,
Glistening with rainbows.

It escaped from the ring
And rose into the air,
Colours swirling its surface,
A dance in the sun.
It wafted higher, she giggled
As it swung on the breeze,
'Til suddenly, it popped,
Raining soap suds in the air.
Startled!
Shocked by the change,
Her face froze for an instant.
'Will she cry now?' I wondered.

Then swiftly reanimated,
She blew another bubble,
And laughed at this wondrous thing.
She clapped her hands, what joy!
To create such beauty, on a whim.

So, this is where I leave you, dear reader. I want to thank you, for whether it is published or not, your virtual presence has been the motivating factor in writing this book. Without you, I doubt I would ever have re-read my poems and discovered the treasures within them and through them, my own spiritual path. It was as if the poems plotted out the stages of gestation of the spiritual foetus I was carrying and only by becoming fully conscious of this process, by sharing it with you, was I able to actualise the spiritual birth they led to. Thank you.

I sincerely hope it has been of value to you.

With love,

Diana

If this book has inspired you in some way and you would like to make contact with me, you can email me here:

camilla462024@outlook.com

PART TWO

Supporting Material

Why and How I Wrote This Book and Insights I Acquired Through Reviewing This Process

Since I finished writing this book, and in the process of editing and refining it, I gained various insights and realisations that I have incorporated into the book and record in the following. One very strong feeling I had was that my whole spiritual journey was supervised and facilitated by my muse, my spiritual guide. My free will was not in any way limited or infringed, but I was not allowed to progress further along the path until certain necessary requirements had been met and that was for my own safety. This is clarified below in my notes on the '*Interim Poems*' for it seems I was not able to progress to Cycle Three, until I had raised my level of consciousness further.

———————————

Writing this book has been a complete revelation to me. The experiences and poems came first, and without understanding why or how it was happening, the transformations I experienced over the next six decades took place anyway.

It was only when confronted with the task of sharing the journey with you, I recognised the need to comprehend the process itself. Thus began the intellectual pursuit – to understand it.

So, faced with over 550 poems, many of which I had not re-read for decades, how was I to create an authentic account of my struggles to survive, and the extraordinary journey which had the effect of peeling away everything in me that was inessential, in order to finally reveal my True Self?

Although I felt whole, embraced and loved by the spiritual world of which I was a part, I felt something else was required of me, a record of this whole spiritual journey, and until that was completed, only then could I feel my journey was finally complete. This feeling was beautifully expressed in a paragraph I came across:

"He knew that in his internal universe, there was a mission etched in a secret language, like drawings on the wall of an ancient cave that gave him his direction and meaning. It could not be altered and it would always be there to guide him to the right path."
(Connelly, M. (2016), p. 385)

I wandered about for several days with the questions 'How do I do this?' and 'What have I learned?' on my mind until my muse took pity on me and suggested I ponder on '*Snow-white and the Seven Dwarfs*'. Was she kidding me? No. So I pondered. She had chosen well, for Walt Disney's film of this name had always been my favourite fairy story.

Any young girl in my generation (1950's) would have loved this film. Pure romance with an idealistic dream of what her life would be like 'once her Prince had come' and kissed her awake, a sweet picture of the innocence of childhood. But what happens then? In psychological terms the male represents the principle of consciousness – our ego, and the period of sweet innocence, of unconsciousness ends, a fact I had registered with the 'Poems of Innocence'. Surely the spiritual journey starts here. ***Except it doesn't!***

Realisation One

Thanks to my muse's suggestion, I was led to reconsider the significance of the years between my birth and age twenty-one. One of the first mistakes I had made was to relegate those years to an unimportant prelude to the 'real story', whereas this is a period of major importance, during which the ego first appears as it struggles out of the sea of unconsciousness. The ego is the instrument for making experience conscious and without it our lives would be pointless.

Realisation Two

Initially I had focused on the Cycles of Poems and discounted the Gaps of time following them. I had it *the wrong way round*, for it was during the **Gap periods** that all the work was done which then produced the following harvest of poems, (a bit like school, when you study for a year and receive the harvest in the results of the exams).

Realisation Three

I thought that once I had produced a collection of poems that I would automatically proceed to the next stage of the journey. However, with Cycle Two, it was not until I had undertaken further training and produced two more lots of poems (the *Interim Poems*) that Cycle Two ended. It appeared that I had to achieve a higher level of consciousness before I was equipped to start on Cycle Three.

It became clear to me that until I was able to consciously accept responsibility for the circumstances of my life and to acknowledge I had consciously chosen my mother and my family – prior to my birth

– that I had attained the level of consciousness that permitted me to proceed to Cycle Three. Had I not attended the three-year training in the Deep Memory Process (Past Life Therapy) with Roger Woolger, I doubt I could have attained that level of awareness.

Realisation Four

Each Cycle of Poems signals a period of development has been achieved. This is then **followed** by a change in life direction / focus:

Poems of Innocence: Change from Science to Arts and Humanities.

Cycle One Poems: Now focussed on developing counselling skills and setting up a counselling service.

Cycle Two Poems: Focus now on everything spiritual – trainings and workshops, including a three year training in Deep Memory Process with Roger Woolger.

The *Interim Poems* were an integral part of Cycle Two and I could not progress to Cycle Three until they had been written: 'Last Confessions', written in 2006 and 'Requiem for Passing Era', written in 2009/10.

Cycle Two completed: Change of focus to acquiring Creative Writing skills.

Cycle Three: Coincided with my retirement from counselling and the closure of the counselling service in 2013. Writing fables and books based on alchemical / spiritual themes now took precedence.

The Poems

The next issue to deal with was how to keep the clarity and integrity of the journey represented in the poems, whilst restricting the number of poems used, which had accumulated over the years.

Poems of innocence:	22 poems over 3 years
Cycle One:	76 poems over 24 years
Cycle Two:	45 poems over 7 years
Interim poems Last Confessions	6 poems over 8 years
Requiem:	3 poems over 3 years
Cycle Three:	73 poems over 13 years

This amounted to a total of 225 poems. This seemed a huge number of poems which might overwhelm the continuity of the narrative. How could I reduce this number without doing damage to the integrity of the journey?

My first decision was to eliminate the Poems of Innocence from this total, as they preceded the actual spiritual journey. This reduced the number of poems to 203, but that was still a large number.

I was then inspired to consider the stages of Alchemy.

ALCHEMY

"The operations of alchemy are stages in an eternal pattern of transformation that is part of the fabric of time and space. This same pattern is within us, as a species slowly moving towards evolutionary perfection and in our personal temperament as well: the inner struggle of our soul buried in matter to unite with spirit in the clear light of higher consciousness."
(Hauck, D.W. (2004), p.181)

The Eight Operations of Alchemy

These refer to the stages incurred in any process of transformation, be that from lead to gold or the spiritual journey. It describes the intermediate stages typical of a process and provided me with a further bit of structure with which to organise the poems. These stages can be described as follows:

Stage One: Awakening to present reality. Recognising changes need to be made.

Stage Two: Emotionally adjusting to adaptations needed.

Stage Three: What to keep, what to jettison. Losses.

Stage Four: Head and heart agree on changes needed. Harmony.

Stage Five: Dark night of Soul. Suffering experienced as changes not yet made. The suffering is a powerful incentive to make the changes.

Stage Six: Rallying of courage and determination to make changes. Hope revives.

Stage Seven: Resuming the process. Possible back-sliding, but you have the courage to resume your efforts.

Stage Eight: Celebrate the changes made, for this nourishes the continuing process.

It was then a matter of going through the poems in each cycle, which were in chronological order and identifying which ones fitted best into these stages.

As the poems were in chronological order, and it was the content of a poem which dictated which stage it belonged to, I didn't have to make any adjustments to fit some preconceived notion of "how it should be", for the spiritual journey is a transformational process and will therefore harmonise with a structure which is also transformational in its trajectory.

What I found was that there were a number of poems which could easily occupy these stages in sequence and it was simply a matter of deciding which of these expressed the stage in the clearest way. In practice I used around three poems for each stage. I felt that around 30 poems would be adequate to cover the part of the spiritual journey that a particular cycle was covering.

This enabled me to reduce the number of poems needed from 225 to 102, whilst still including the Interim Poems. This number Ensured that there were adequate numbers of appropriate poems to carry the narrative forward without overwhelming the reader.

Having dealt with the number of poems to be used, I turned my attention to other structural elements which might assist the reader in following the narrative.

Preludes

I referred earlier to the GAP periods which intersperse the cycles of poems. These are the periods when extensive work was done to increase my level of consciousness, which subsequently led through to a further cycle of poems.

I felt it was important to keep the reader up-to-date with what I had been doing during the GAP periods to gain further experience. So, I introduced a prelude before each new cycle of poems. Their purpose was to familiarise the reader with my state of mind as I began the next part of my journey. These included important experiences, trainings and any changes in circumstances that would set the scene for the next cycle of poems.

Analysis of the Meaning of the Poems

Following the narrative of the spiritual journey through poems is not the easiest way to do it, but I could think of no other way to share the journey in its full authenticity, than to offer the poems that informed and guided my path, however difficult some of them might be to read.

As not everyone is familiar with reading poetry, I decided to add an analysis of what each poem meant to me, at the end of each cycle.

Commentary

I later realised that knowing what each poem meant in isolation gives no indication of the progress made. This only becomes apparent when the trajectory of a whole cycle of poems is considered. I have, therefore, added a commentary on the progress in spiritual growth as the last element in each cycle.

Synopsis

Sharing my spiritual journey through poems is an authentic way to share the journey, but it is piece-meal and not a smooth narrative. I felt that providing a synopsis – a summary of the whole journey would enable a reader to accommodate the inevitable 'jumps' in the narrative.

Direction of the Journey as a whole

Now that I had a basic structure for the narrative, I wanted to consider other versions of spiritual journeys to see if they could throw some light on the trajectory – direction of the journey as a whole. I found four versions, including Jung's Individuation Process, but I wanted ones which also had a similar tripartite structure which related to the Three Cycles so prominent in my book. I therefore selected the following:

Dante's Divine Comedy in which there are three scenes:

a. Hell – the Inferno. b. Purgation and c. Paradise.

Gnostic Initiations in which there are three classifications for potential initiates.

The Alchemical Process in which three full passes through its eight operations are required to achieve ultimate success – termed the *Philosopher's Stone*, equated with enlightenment.

I decided to explore each of these to see if they could offer something useful with regard to their characteristic tripartite nature, which might throw some light on our picture of the spiritual journey so far.

1. DANTE'S DIVINE COMEDY

This is a narrative poem and the main theme is the spiritual journey of man through life. He learns about the nature of sin and its consequences during his experiences through the three realms of Hell, Purgatory and Paradise. The goal of Dante is to reach spiritual maturity and an understanding of God's Love.

I felt these three realms mirrored well the characteristics of the three cycles entitled 'A Lost Soul Seeking Direction', 'Confronting my Demons and coming to terms with my Shadow', and 'Recognising the Ego and then Surrendering it.'

2. THE GNOSTICS AND INITIATION

The Gnostics were explorers of consciousness who generated a mystical philosophy which promised experiential knowledge of truth. They categorised human beings at *three* levels according to their level of self-awareness.

Hylics or Materialists:

This group identified themselves with their bodies. They tended not to think about God at all or have a religious relationship with what they imagined to be the ultimate authority figure.

Psychics or Spiritists:

This group of initiates understood self-knowledge to be about examining their faults and failings so that they could become better people. Personal growth was achieved by working on themselves. They had a softer conception of God as a wise parent who nurtures us on our personal journey through life's trials and tribulations, enabling a relationship of love, devotion and friendship.

Pneumatics:

Pneumatics became aware of themselves as spirit or consciousness. The pneumatic or spirit initiation is about coming to understand that we are not a person at all. We are impersonal spirit or consciousness. They no longer imagine God as a big person, but in impersonal terms such as the 'One' or the 'Good'.

(Summarised from Freke, T. and Gandy, P. (2001) p. 72)

How do these different levels of Initiation relate to my Journey?

I could definitely identify with the changes in my perceptions of God as I progressed through my journey. As a child I had felt alienated towards the image of God as presented by my local church. An authoritarian presence I could not relate to, similar to that of the **Hylic – Materialists.**

When I established the connection with my muse/spiritual guide, this changed my feelings about the spiritual world, for I experienced her love and guidance as evidence of God's love. Initially, I called her my 'second mother', very much like the **Psychic-Spiritist's** conception of God.

My eventual experience of being part of the 'All' relates to the conception of the **Pneumatics.**

3. **ALCHEMY:** The alchemists believed that ultimate success came in *three passes* through the eight operations. The successful completion of each cycle of eight operations is called a Magisterium.

First Magisterium:

This represents gaining control and perfecting the life force as it is expressed in the body, so that the alchemist might live long enough to complete the Great Work in one lifetime.

Second Magisterium:

This is achieved when the mind is perfectly controlled and directed through the willpower, so that fear, ego and other psychological baggage does not interfere with the full expression of the power of the mind.

Third Magisterium:

This is seen as the perfection of the physical body on the spiritual plane, forming the Astral Body – the spiritual body.

The three Magisteriums focused on developing different aspects of the individual, first the body and instincts, then the mind and will-power and lastly the spirit.

Conclusion:

In spite of their different terminologies, all three of these different models of the spiritual journey agreed that the direction of travel was to deal with issues around the Body and Instincts, then the Mind and lastly the Spirit. This reassured me that the trajectory of my own spiritual journey was in line with other versions of this human experience.

———————

What I was aware of, was that in sharing my Journey, I had focused very little on the body.

I then realised that in the Introduction to this book the circumstances around my early life and the adaptations required for me to optimise my life are well covered. I felt that the 'Material / Body' issue (that was a characteristic of the three models), related to that earliest period of life in which we are coming to terms with 'being born as a human' and adjusting to the circumstances, in the family, society and culture in which we are born. It is these factors which provide us with the material that is subsequently dealt with psychologically, in the mind, and then spiritually. Probably the most significant issue is that it is the period where the Ego is being formed, which is essential to engage in the following parts of the journey.

———————

There are a number of elements which are not clearly common to all the models used (although they may be implicit in them).

Metanoia of the Gnostics:

According to their philosophy, the whole process begins when an individual experiences a turning point in their life, where they cannot continue to invest in their separate ego because they intuitively know life is actually concerned with spiritual awakening. This point is termed 'metanoia' meaning a 'change of heart'.

I had no trouble in identifying this as the time when I turned my back on science as a career and changed direction. It was also the moment when my muse came into my life for the second time – fourteen years after her first breakthrough into my consciousness.

THE FINAL GOAL

Alchemy:

'The goal of alchemy is not to remain in the realm of spirit...but to become purified in the realm of spirit and then <u>return to the earth</u> as SEEDS OF SPIRIT'. (Hauck, D.W. (2004) p. 203)

Zen:

This idea is more clearly expressed in the final stage of the Ten Oxherding pictures. This is a Zen idea and the version I am most familiar with is in the 'Guidebook to Zen and the Art of Motorcycle Maintenance by Robert Pirsig'. (DiSanto, R.L. and Steele, T.J. (1990) p. 48)

Final stage of Ten Oxherding pictures:
'Awakened enlightenment takes the form of a fat jolly rustic, who wanders from village to village, from mundane situation to mundane situation. Having attained enlightenment...*he returns fully to the human world'.*

TRUE SELF

The most important refinement I made, was to the definition of the True Self, to be found in the introduction. The True Self is also termed the Psyche and the Soul and hence is the goal of the journey I am considering in this book. The current definition is comprehensive and its importance as the goal in life becomes clear.

———————————

What about the rest of the poems?

Observant readers may wonder what happened to the rest of the 550 poems I mentioned in paragraph 2 of this chapter. It is clear that only 225 were used to structure the narrative of the spiritual journey as far as the end of Cycle Three, but the spiritual journey does not end there, as I will clarify later. The later stages of spiritual development are termed the INDIVIDUATION process and this is described fully in Chapters 14 and 15. Poems continued to inform this later stage of development.

Chapter Twelve

Balancing the Rational and Irrational Functions of the Brain

There were three reasons why I felt this issue was an important consideration:

1.   Awareness of my own straight-jacketed rational bias.

In Chapter Eighteen I have described the reason Cycle One took twenty-four years. My right-hand brain functions had been neglected in my school education and as both sides of the brain have to be functioning well before much progress can be made in the psycho-spiritual journey, I had to focus on developing the functions of the right side of my brain, so that there was a balance between the left side rational analytical processes and the right side aesthetic synthetic ones.

2.   Mentoring for this project.

It felt important to me that I seek advice and feedback from professionals on this project. I therefore approached a Jungian analyst for help on the academic material and a professional poet for his input on the poetry side.

The analyst would have nothing to do with the book once he discovered that poetry was involved.

The professional poet was of the opinion that the poems needed tightening with regard to expression and form. He noted that 'Yeats revised a poem fifty times in order that it *appear genuine and spontaneous*'! It is difficult to imagine poems that were more genuine and spontaneous than the ones that erupted from my unconscious through the agency of my Muse/Spiritual Guide.

I recognise that my poems or verse-like forms may be less than perfect, but the content is what is important and I hope I have communicated that adequately.

The reaction of these two people underlines the problem of specialisation such that one is either *primarily* an academic with a rational bias or a creative artist with an aesthetic irrational bias.

3. Academic Corroboration

The following are excerpts from academic studies which focus on this weakness in our educational system and the psychological consequences of those shortfalls.

'...ever since the Renaissance, stress has increasingly been laid on the need to develop left hemispheric functions at the expense of the right. Encouragement of the left hemisphere begins early in life with the emphasis placed in all Western primary schools on the need for proficiency in the three 'R's (writing, reading and arithmetic). Although right hemispheric activities such as art, drama, dancing and music are given a place in the curriculum, fewer resources and fewer hours are allocated to them than to left-sided disciplines such as mathematics, languages, physics and chemistry; and at times of economic retrenchment, it is invariably the right-sided activities which are pruned or curtailed.

Education reflects the ruling obsessions of a society; and a culture such as ours which stresses the importance of rational, analytic processes rather than aesthetic, synthetic ones, and which places a higher value on material achievement than on symbolic expression, inevitably promotes a form of left hemispheric 'imperialism'.........(this) has been mirrored by a macrocosmic imperialism on a global scale, where a right-wing, 'left hemispheric' oligarchy imposes its will on the

increasingly left-wing 'subdominant' peoples of the world.'
(Stevens, A. (1982) p255-256)

Jung agreed that neurosis was self-division. The purpose of therapy was to heal the split.
(Jung, C. (1953) C.W. 7 para. 428)

The *'merely conscious'* man he saw as *'all ego'* a mere fragment inasmuch as he exists *'apart from the unconscious'*.
(Jung, C. (1953) C.W.12 para. 42)

Healing is wholeness and *'conscious wholeness consists in a successful union of ego and Self (unconscious), so that both preserve their intrinsic qualities'*.
(Jung, C. (2014) C.W. 8 paras 195-6)

'Disalliance with the unconscious is synonymous with loss of instinct and rootlessness. If we can successfully develop that function which I have called transcendent, the disharmony ceases and we can then enjoy the favourable side of the unconscious. The unconscious then gives us all the encouragement and help that a bountiful nature can shower upon a man.'
(Jung, C. (1953) C.W. 7, paras 195-6)

'The evolutionary stratification of the psyche is more clearly discernible in the dream than in the conscious mind. In the dream, the psyche speaks in images, and gives expression to instincts, which derive from the most primitive levels of nature. Therefore, through the assimilation of unconscious contents, the momentary life of consciousness can once more be brought into harmony with the law of nature from which it all too easily departs, and the patient can be led back to the natural law of his own being.'
Jung, C. (1954) C.W. 16, para 351.

'*Dreams, therefore, are the language used in the life-long dialogue proceeding nightly between the ego and the self: they are the means by which the individual becomes psychically related to the life-cycle of his species. Jung was the first psychologist to draw attention to the importance of dream-series in mediating and exemplifying this process. Taken singly, each dream compensation...*'
Stevens, A. (1982) p. 271)

'*...is a momentary adjustment of one-sidedness or an equalisation of disturbed balance. But with deeper insight and experience, these apparently separate acts of compensation arrange themselves into a kind of plan. They seem to hang together and in the deepest sense to be subordinated to a common goal, so that a long dream-series no longer appears as a senseless string of incoherent and isolated happenings, but resembles the successive steps in a planned and orderly process of development. I have called this unconscious process spontaneously expressing itself in the symbolism of a long dream-series* **the individuation process.**'
(Jung, C. (2014) C.W. 8, para 550)

───────────

Let us look at this issue from a scientific point of view. Robert Monroe founded the Monroe Institute dedicated to education, exploration, and research into practical methods of accelerated learning through expanded forms of consciousness, in the 1950's. In his final book '*Ultimate Journey*', on page 88, he stated:

'*The trick is to get both left and right brains into simultaneous and synchronous action.....you should never abandon one for the other.*'

Chapter Thirteen

Where Did the Poems Come From?

The Transcendent Function

At the time, the most puzzling thing about the poems was how I managed to convert a tension in my body into a poem. I didn't dwell on this, for the benefit I got was a relief from the uncomfortable tension I had been feeling, like letting off steam, a safety valve.

I learned to interpret the tension in my body as a summons to 'pay attention' and I wrote down the poems, a bit like taking dictation. I had no idea what the poem would be about until I had written it down and could read it.

Decades later, when I came to write this book my curiosity about this process was peeked and I set about researching how such a process came about. The first breakthrough was when I came across the following quote in a book:

> *"The basic proposition is this: An unconscious symbol is lived but not perceived. The dynamism of the unconscious symbol is experienced only as a wish or an urgency towards some external action. The image behind the urgency is not seen."*
> *(Edinger, F. (1972) p.113)*

So, the urgency I experienced to get somewhere safe to 'give birth' is explained, but how then could the tension be converted into words, forming a meaningful poem? To understand this, I had to do some more research and I learned about the Transcendent Function.

"Jung considered the transcendent function to be the most significant factor in psychological process. He insisted that its intervention was due to the conflict between the opposites." (And the tension created - My words.)
(Samuels, A. (1986) p. 150)

It is a psychological mechanism that unites the opposites and helps bring the Self into manifestation. It is a capacity in the psyche which includes both the ego (consciousness) and the unconscious:

"The Transcendent Function cannot proceed through reason, because reason acknowledges no ambiguity: truth is not falsehood, white is not black, everything is one thing or the other. But when permitted to do so the psyche transcends reason and the rules of logic, no less than the opposites, for it sees no problem in the simultaneous perception of incompatibilities."
(Stevens, A. (1982) p. 242)

Okay, so far. There is a bridge, the Transcendent Function, in the psyche which is able to unite my urgency towards action – with the ego which has the capacity to write.

"To affect a union of opposites, the contents of the unconscious must be joined with the ego, so as to create a third position. Because the Transcendent Function arises from the union of conscious and unconscious contents, it creates a third position."
(Raff, J. (2000) p. 17)

So, what is this third position?

"That which is capable of uniting these two is a metaphorical statement (the symbol)."
(Samuels, A. (1986) p. 150)

That's all very well, but how is this symbol translated into a poem?

"The Transcendent Function resides in the mutual influence of consciously and unconscious, ego and Self, and Jung believed that there were two basic methods by which this mutuality could be brought about: 'the way of creative formulation' (e.g. active imagination, creative phantasy, dream, symbols, art and aesthetics) and 'the way of understanding' (e.g. intellectual concepts, verbal formulations, conscious awareness and abstraction."
(Stevens, A. (1982) p. 272)

Writing of these two approaches, Jung declared:

"One tendency seems to be the regulating principle of the other; both are bound together in a compensatory relationship....aesthetic formulation needs understanding of the meaning, and understanding needs aesthetic formulation. The two supplement each other to form the transcendent function."
(Jung's C.W. 8, quoted by Rossi, (1977) p. 45)

The symbol, through the mechanism of the Transcendent Function, has to present itself in such a way that it has an artistic form as well as offering the meaning implicit in the symbol. Thus, we arrive at the poems.

But why poems and not, say, a painting, a sculpture? In exploring this question, I came across a quote by Otto Rank in his book Art and Artist that "poetry is the language of the soul". As it is the soul, the unconscious, via my muse that is the active partner in delivering the information to me, it therefore makes sense that she would use poems.

Chapter Fourteen

Comparing the two Theoretical Models Used

Although these are not directly apparent in Part One, they coloured my thinking throughout the writing of this book.

The Individuation Process

This is a psychological process. The goal is to enable the individual to create the Self. The Self is the centre of the Psyche / Soul, which is defined as:

'totality of all psychic processes, conscious as well as unconscious'
(Jung, C. (1921) para. 797)

To clarify what the Individuation Process is, I need to refer to Jung's work on dreams and I will take extracts from two quotes:

'Dreams, therefore, are the language used in the life-long dialogue proceeding nightly between the ego and the self: they are the means by which the individual becomes psychically related to the life-cycle of his species….. taken singly each dream compensation…'
(Stevens, A. (1982) p.271)

and:

'is a momentary adjustment of one-sidedness or an equalization of disturbed balance. But with deeper insight and experience, these apparently separate acts of compensation arrange themselves into a kind of plan. They seem to hang together and in the deepest sense to be subordinated to a common goal, so that a long series no longer appears as a senseless string of incoherent and isolated happenings, but resembles the successive steps in a planned and orderly process of development. I have called this unconscious process spontaneously expressing itself in the symbolism of a long dream-series the

individuation process.'
(Jung, C. (1960) para. 550)

The sequence of poems I accumulated over my life time are similar to the long dream series Jung recognised as describing the *'successive steps in planned and orderly process of development'* and it is this gradual transformation over time as recorded in the poems, which reveals itself as the spiritual journey.

An advantage of Jung's model is that it provides a lexicon of archetypes (innate psychological structures) that may be encountered during the deeper stages of this psychological process. For example, the Wise Woman, the Muse, the Goddess, the Mother and the Adversary.

Personal experiences will tend to colour our interaction with them, but the archetypes are primordial images in the unconscious, have manifold meanings and a limitless wealth of references. They have enormous power, carrying a strong charge of potentially overpowering energy which is difficult to resist. This is why it is so important to develop a strong ego before encountering these archetypes.

Jung regarded the True Self as the goal of his Individuation Process. He also believed the Alchemists' Philosopher's Stone was a symbol for the Self. His reasons for this are set out in Appendix A.

'This comparison of the Self with the Philosopher's Stone united Jung's model with the Alchemical one. He was able to explore the spiritual ideas of the alchemist as they related to his own religious perspective.'
(Raff, J. (2000) p.3)

The Spiritual Alchemical Process

This is a metaphysical/philosophical model in its classical mode, the goal of which was to create the Philosopher's Stone. It has been applied to the Spiritual transformation of human beings. One advantage is that it divides the transformation process into eight stages.

I have set these stages out in Chapter 11 but I include them here for ease of reference. I also include the Alchemical Names of the Stages and the slightly different descriptions.

THE EIGHT STAGES OF EACH CYCLE

Alchemical Name	Key Words	Meaning
Stage One Calcination	Incinerating the Ego's present reality. Burning off the dross	Awakening to control. Recognition that changes need to be made.
Stage Two Dissolution	Redeeming emotion and intuition Learning to let go	Emotionally adjusting to adaptations needed.
Stage Three Separation	Learning to discriminate and developing wisdom	What to keep and what to jettison.
Stage Four Conjunction	Balancing inner masculine and inner feminine	Your head and heart agree and you resolve to make changes.

Stage Five Putrefaction	Dark Night of the Soul Learning how to allow limiting beliefs to die	You have yet to make changes and hence are in the hell of your current situation. The suffering experienced can be the powerful incentive to make the changes needed.
Stage Six Fermentation	Integrating lower levels of consciousness with the higher.	Rallying of determination and courage to implement changes. Hope revives.
Stage Seven Distillation	Refining the True Self	Possible back-sliding but you have the courage to resume your efforts.
Stage Eight Coagulation	Wholeness and Happiness	Celebrate the changes made for this nourishes the continuing process.

The Alchemical Process requires three cycles of the eight stages throughout the life of the individual. Each of these cycles of 8 stages is called a Magisterium. The three Magisteriums are necessary as life circumstances change over time and the individual matures. The following is a brief description of what each one achieves:-

First Cycle: Achieves a working relationship between the ego / conscious mind and the unconscious. The Self is still being developed and is described as Latent.

Second Cycle: Makes the union between the ego / conscious mind and the unconscious permanent. The Self is described as Manifest.

Third Cycle: Unites the Manifest Self with a centre that transcends the human psyche, a centre one might call Divine.

I need to clarify something here: The Soul is personal and unique to each one of us. The task of Cycle One and Two is that of personal transformation with the goal of becoming conscious of the contents of the Soul and then uniting the Ego and Soul to create the True Self – the Manifest Self.

The Spirit is transpersonal. The task that the Manifest Self is confronted with as it enters the Third Cycle is that of surrendering its will to the Greater Will of the Spirit. It is about personal transcendence and the ultimate realisation of the Oneness of All That Is, which is accompanied by the experience of all-embracing love.

Chapter Fifteen

The Unique Contribution of each Theoretical Model

Jung's Process provides understanding, purpose and meaning, whereas Alchemy provides structure to the individuation process and also a more transpersonal overview of the journey.

Understanding:

Carl Jung's Individuation Process is helpful in that it provides an overall rationale for engaging in the long process of self-exploration and of recording the experiences undergone. He states:

>'A long series no longer appears as a senseless string of incoherent and isolated happenings, but resemble the successive steps in a planned and orderly process of development.'
>(Jung, C. (1960) para. 550)

It is this gradual development and transformation over time which is recorded in my poems and reveals itself as the spiritual journey.

Framework for Organising the Poems:

The Alchemical Process offers a structure within which the poems can be seen to be part of the process mentioned above. Each stage is characterised by a shift in focus of the individual.

Stage One: An attitude of willingness to confront what is going wrong in one's life is the starting point here and a consideration of what that might mean in practical terms.

Stage Two: These potential changes are evaluated here in emotional and feeling terms.

Stage Three: Consideration of the actual changes that need to be made are clarified here. What to keep as it serves the individual and what needs to be got rid of.

Stage Four: This stage is reached when the mental decisions made are buttressed by emotional support and agreement. A state of harmony exists.

Stage Five: It can be a bit overwhelming and depressing to come down to earth and realise that the resolution of Stage Four has not yet been actualised and one is still in the original mess. Yet the suffering experienced here may be exactly what is required to mobilise the effort to take the steps needed to move beyond the status quo.

Stage Six: Determination and courage to effect the changes needed accumulate, and hope builds, as the goal is kept in mind and the benefits are recognised and anticipated.

Stage Seven: As resolutions are put into effect some of the benefits begin to feed through and stimulate the ongoing effort. Back-sliding is a useful reminder that determination and resolve have to be nurtured.

Stage Eight: Success in achieving the goal is accompanied by a growing sense of empowerment and confidence in one's ability to achieve whatever goals one sets oneself.

These stages are generic and are expressed in neutral terms, so they can be applied to all the Three Cycles of the Alchemical Process. These stages may take many years to complete during which psychological or spiritual changes are being made.

The Three Magisteriums describe what is to be achieved in each of the cycles:

Magisterium One: Gaining control and perfecting the life force as it is expressed in the body.

MagisteriumTwo: Mastery of the mind so that it is perfectly controlled and directed through the will power, so that fear, ego and other psychological baggage does not interfere in the full expression of the power of the mind.

MagisteriumThree: The perfection of the physical body on the spiritual plane, thus forming the astral or spiritual body

Cycle One and Two are concerned with psychological growth and development. Cycle Three is focused on spiritual awakening and development.

Chapter Sixteen

Why Three Cycles?

There are three cycles necessary to accomplish the goal, whether described as the Self or the Philosopher's Stone. These cycles represent three levels at which opposites unite. In Cycles One and Two the opposites uniting are the ego and the unconscious soul and produce the Manifest Self. This is a psychological process. In Cycle Three, the opposites uniting are the Manifest Self and a level of reality that transcends it which may be called Divine. It is a spiritual process.

Each cycle may be separated by years. During the Gap periods in my journey, I worked hard gaining life experiences and furthering my understanding and growth through trainings, psychotherapy, travel and other activities. These provided the extra material to facilitate my spiritual development, which would in turn provide the inspiration to inform the next cycle of poems.

FIRST CYCLE:

This begins when the ego discovers the reality of the unconscious and makes an effort to pay attention to it. Beginning with its own dreams, the ego attempts to gain some insight into the nature of the unconscious and to listen to its messages. In my case, I was informed by the poems which erupted from my unconscious. I had no idea what these would be about until I read them on the page. They provided me with awareness of the emotions and feelings that I had repressed into the unconscious and which needed action if I was to develop psychologically. This integration of unconscious material with my conscious mind meant I was creating the True Self throughout my journey.

SECOND CYCLE:

The Self progresses to such a degree that it takes on a life and reality of its own within the psyche. At the same time, the ego experiences a profound transformation and comes to realise itself as part of the Manifest Self. At this second level, all the work performed during the first cycle comes to fruition in a deeper revolution that binds the unconscious and the ego in an indissoluble union termed the Manifest Self. The individuation process has entered a stage that is ongoing but stable.

THIRD CYCLE:

The Manifest Self comes into contact with a level of reality that transcends it. This elevation into the third cycle can be facilitated by the individual engaging in spiritual practices, such as:

Meditation,

Prayer,

Yoga,

Reading inspirational material,

Attending meetings / conferences on relevant subjects,

Trusting in the power of life to guide you,

Most of all, **being Love in action**.

The individual soul is dependent on the spiritual world for its very existence and has to trust that its need for transcendence is recognised and nurtured. Once your soul has had contact with the spiritual world, there is no end to the relationship and your joy in the union sustains and guides your life.

Chapter Seventeen

The Difference in the Lengths of the Cycles

It will be noted that Cycle One took twenty-four years to work through the 8 stages of the process, whereas Cycle Two took around seventeen years including the two lots of *Interim Poems*. Cycle Three took around three years to produce the last collection of poems. However spiritual development never ceases and in a sense the journey never ends.

Cycle One: The reason for this long period is that as I approached Cycle One my psychological and intellectual development was extremely unbalanced. Most of the activities I had focussed on during my first twenty-one years were analytical, logical and rational – left hand brain functions.

This imbalance was naturally corrected as I became attracted to all those areas of development so far neglected, art, drama, dancing and music, all feeling based aesthetic activities, non-rational and right-hand brain functions.

This rebalancing was necessary to facilitate the subsequent interaction of both sides of the brain, a characteristic of eventual wholeness. In alchemy this is referred to as the *Marriage of the Sun and Moon* – symbolising the two ways of knowing and experiencing the world.

Cycle Two was preceded by a gap of seven years and it was during this gap period that the hard work was done that culminated in the transformations recorded in the poems. However, further training and experience were needed before I was able to engage in

Cycle Three. The three-year training in the 'Deep Memory Process' (Past Life Therapy) I undertook with Roger Woolger enabled me to attain the level of consciousness needed to proceed further. Two lots of poems – the '*Interim Poems*' describe the changes I had needed. In all it took around seventeen years to complete Cycle Two.

Cycle Three was preceded by a gap of two years during which many changes were made and subsequently recorded in the poems. What is clearly evident is that the tone of the poems change, they are now transpersonal in nature. Spiritual development never ends, so although passage through the three stages was achieved, I am still working through the distillation stage of this Cycle.

Chapter Eighteen

Cycles, Gaps, Preludes and Stages

How do I know when a new Cycle begins?

The harvest of poems comes at the end of a Cycle. A new Cycle begins as soon as the harvest of poems from the previous Cycle has been garnered.

The Gaps between Cycles

These are the periods of time when all the hard work is done. Before each Cycle begins, I will provide brief information on what I had done to facilitate the ongoing process during these Gap periods. The poems in the eight stages are the results of that work.

Preludes

At the beginning of each Cycle there is a Prelude. Their purpose is to situate the reader in my inner world as I begin the next part of the journey. Brief details of any trainings and important experiences will set the scene.

How do I know when a Stage changes?

The content of the poems themselves dictate which Stage they belong to.

Chapter Nineteen

Structure Employed in Part One of the Book

Age:	0 – 21 (1946 – 1965)
Prelude:	The Introduction performs this function.
Function:	Development of the Ego.
Harvest:	'Poems of Innocence'.
Change of Direction:	From Science to Arts and the Humanities.

CYCLE ONE BEGINS:

Age:	22 – 46 (1965 – 1989)
No Prelude:	My life proceeded in a different direction immediately.
Function:	1. To develop the RHS of my brain (the irrational) by engaging in a wide range of activities.
	2. To produce poems that informed my journey and work on personal unconscious material and become aware of archetypal figures.
Harvest:	Poems 'Lost Soul Seeking Direction(1992 - 1968) .'
Change of Direction:	Personal development combined with trainings to become a counsellor.

GAP OF 7 YEARS before CYCLE TWO BEGINS

Age:	46 – 53 (1992 – 1999)
Prelude:	To set scene for new cycle.

Function:	Major confrontation with Archetypes. Starting to Integrate Ego and Unconscious.
Harvest:	Poems 'Confronting my Demons and Coming to terms with my Shadow'.
Change of Direction:	Focus now more on spiritual development.

GAP OF 7 YEARS before the INTERIM POEMS:

These are an integral part of Cycle Two. An Increase in consciousness was achieved during the three year training in Deep Memory Process with Roger Woolger between 2004 – 2006.

Interim Poems:

Age:	53 – 60 (1999 – 2006)
Prelude:	This covers one group of the *Interim Poems*.
Function:	To deepen my level of consciousness.
Harvest:	Poems 'Last Confessions.(2006) '
Change of Direction:	Focus on wide range of spiritual workshops and trainings, bridging psychotherapy and spiritual disciplines.

GAP OF 3 YEARS before the second group of *Interim Poems*

Age:	61 – 64 (2006 – 2009/10)
Function:	To mature and stabilise my level of consciousness.
Harvest:	Poems 'Requiem for a Passing Era.(2010 – 2009) '

Change of Direction:	Recognition of our responsibility towards the natural world Training in Permaculture and Sustainability issues.

GAP OF 2 YEARS before CYCLE THREE BEGINS.

Age:	64 – ongoing (2010 – ongoing).
Prelude:	To set scene for the Third Cycle.
Function:	To engage with a Transpersonal level of consciousness.
Harvest:	Poems: 'Recognising the Ego and Surrendering it.' (2012-13).
Change of Direction:	I retired from counselling and my focus turned to learning creative writing skills.

At the end of this cycle, I had concluded the spiritual journey as far as necessary to provide a route map of how to attain spiritual awakening. In reality the journey never ends.

Chapter Twenty

Outline of the Stages in the Spiritual Journey

1. The development of a strong Ego.

2. Our Western Education System favours the development of the rational mind over the irrational side. Rebalancing this is necessary to enable the integration of the two sides that is necessary during spiritual development

3. Confronting and integrating the contents of the personal unconscious.

4. During later stages of the spiritual journey archetypal figures will need to be confronted and integrated. A strong Ego is essential to avoid being overwhelmed by these extremely powerful entities.

5. Once a working alliance has been formed between the Ego and the Soul, the Self becomes manifest.

6. The Self then has to be refined in order that a second 'marriage' can occur between the Soul and Spirit.

Why did Jung believe the Philosopher's Stone was a Symbol for the Self?

1. He conceived of the Self as the union of opposites and the centre of the psyche.

   The Stone was the union of opposites and often portrayed as centre.

2. The Self could be personified as an inner figure.

   So could the Stone.

3. The Self was the repository of wisdom.

   So too was the Stone.

4. The Self was the goal of all psychic life and the end state to which the Individuation Process led.

   The Stone was the goal of all alchemical endeavours and the end to which all the alchemical processes led.

5. Jung thought that the Self, created symbols in order to make its attributes known.

   The Stone was one such image.

The comparison of the Self with the Stone united Jung's model with the Alchemical one. He was able to explore the spiritual ideas of the alchemist as they related to his own religious perspective. (Raff, J. (2000) p. 3.)

Appendix 'B'

DEFINITIONS

More than one may be provided to ensure clarity.

ALCHEMY: A symbolic representation of the Individuation process. (see Philosophers' Stone).

ANIMUS: An archetype that represents universal masculine characteristics.

The unconscious masculine component of the female psyche.

ARCHETYPES: They are universal inborn models of people's behaviours or personalities that play a role in influencing human behaviour.

Archaic forms of innate human knowledge passed down from our ancestors.

CREATIVE The faculty by which new, uncommon ideas emerge, especially through IMAGINATION.

When emergence does not seem explicable by the mere combination of existing ideas.

The operations of the creative imagination are sometimes explained by the interaction of dormant or non-conscious elements with active conscious thoughts. (Amer. Psychol. Assoc.)

EGO: The centre of consciousness.

FALSE SELF: The False Self is a defensive façade, behind which the person can feel empty, the behaviours being learnt and controlled rather than spontaneous and genuine. Whereas the True Self refers to a sense of self, based on authentic experience, and the feeling of being truly present and alive.

FANTASY vs.
IMAGINATION:
Imagination is often based on real experiences, or a person's experience of their own reality. Fantasy is an unrealistic by-product of the imagination.

Imagination exists in the perfect spirit and is a spiritual function, while Fantasy exists in the body without the perfect spirit.

Fantasy belongs to the physical world and is divorced from deeper truths.

Fantasy creates illusion and folly.

Imagination creates liberation and healing power.

GESTALT:
Refers to the form or shape of something and suggests that the whole is greater than the sum of the parts.

GUARDIAN OF
THE THRESHOLD:
This refers to a spectral image which manifests itself as soon as 'the student of the spirit' ascends upon the path into the higher worlds of knowledge.

A spiritual being which is the sum total of all our past karma, has to be faced and passed before we can know the deepest truth. It holds

	back those who cannot face it and understand it.
INDIVIDUATION PROCESS:	The successive steps in a planned and orderly process of development – an unconscious process that expresses itself in symbols. The True Self is the goal of this process.
INFLATION:	Refers to an identification with the collective psyche caused by an invasion of unconscious archetypal contents. It causes disorientation accompanied by a feeling of immense power and uniqueness or a sense of non-worth and being of no account. The former represents a hypomanic state; the latter depression.
METANOIA:	A term used by the Gnostics meaning a 'change of heart'. It refers to a turning point in the life of an individual, when they cannot continue to invest in their separate ego, because they intuitively know that life is concerned with spiritual awakening.
MIRACLE:	An extraordinary and welcome event that is not explicable by known natural or scientific laws and is therefore attributed to a divine agency.
PARADIGM:	A typical example or pattern or something. A model.

PHILOSOPHERS' STONE (1):	It was the central symbol of the mystical terminology of alchemy, symbolising perfection at its finest, enlightenment and heavenly bliss.
PHILOSOPHERS' STONE (2)	A mythical alchemical substance capable of turning base metals such as mercury into gold and silver.
POSSESSION:	Take-over or occupation of the EGO-personality by some archetypal content. The individual is thus deprived of choice and is powerless to dispose of his WILL.
PROJECTION:	Difficult emotions and unacceptable parts of the personality may be located in a person or object external to the subject. The problematic content is thereby controlled and the individual feels a (temporary) release and sense of well-being. Aspects of the personality sensed to be good and valuable may be projected so as to protect them from the ravages of the rest of the personality, fantasised as bad or destructive.
PSYCHE:	The totality of all psychic processes, conscious as well as unconscious. Also termed the Soul or the True Self
TRUE SELF:	The centre of the Soul created by uniting the conscious and the unconscious mind. Before

unification it is said to be Latent.

Once unified it is said to be Manifest.

SHADOW: An unconscious aspect of the personality that the conscious ego does not identify with.

The entirety of the unconscious.

Everything of which a person is not fully conscious.

SOUL: An alternative word for the Psyche. It is unique to each individual, and therefore personal. The butterfly is often used as a symbol of it.

SPIRIT: The non-material aspect of man. It can neither be described or defined. It is Infinite, Spaceless, Formless and Imageless.

Used to refer to the non-material aspect of a living person such as thought, intention and ideal.

An incorporeal being detached from a human body.

It is the opposite of matter. It is not personal. It lives of itself – neither subject to our human expectations nor the demands of the will or ego. It arrives unbidden.

Jung links spirit with purpose and a kind of intuitive force which connects and influences disparate events and endeavours (see synchronicity and miracles.)

The intervention of so-called spirit seems to demand an increase in consciousness.

SPIRITUAL JOURNEY:
A very individual and intimate quest to consciously deepen insight about life, including a search for purpose and meaning. In general, a spiritual journey describes the process of a person embarking on a quest to deepen their knowledge, understanding and wisdom about themselves, the world and /or God.

SYMBOL:
It is not logical, but encapsulates the psychological situation. Its nature is paradoxical and it represents a third factor or possibility that does not exist in logic, but provides a perspective from which a synthesis of opposing elements can be made.

It attracts our attention to another position, which if appropriately understood, adds to existing personality as well as resolving the conflict.

It is an unconscious invention in answer to a conscious problem.

They are indistinct, metaphoric and enigmatic portrayals of psychic reality.

They are not allegorical for they would then be about something already familiar, but they are expressive of something intensely alive, one might say a stirring in the soul (see Transcendent Function).

SYNCHRONICITY: The simultaneous occurrence of events which appear significantly related but have no discernible causal connection.

A concept introduced by Carl Jung.

A series of signs or events too thought-provoking or emotionally touching to be just coincidence. It is defined as a meaningful coincidence – an event on the outside that speaks to something on the inside – as opposed to just a random occurrence.

TRANSCENDENT FUNCTION: It is a capacity in the psyche which includes both the ego (consciousness) and the unconscious.

The Transcendent Function cannot proceed through reason because reason acknowledges no ambiguity: truth is not falsehood, white is not black, everything is one thing or another. But when permitted to do so the psyche transcends reason and the rules of logic, no less than the opposites, for it sees no problem in the simultaneous perception of incompatibilities. (See 'Where did the poems come from?')

(Definitions from multiple sources, including online.)

Appendix 'C'

Bibliography

Alexander, E. (2012), **Proof of Heaven**. Piatkus, Great Britain.

Buber, M. (1923) **I-Thou.** First published in English in 1937. In 2004 published by Bloomsbury Publishing Plc.

Connelly, M. (2016) **The Wrong Side of Goodbye.** Orion Pub. Group, London.

Deikman, A.J. (1982), **The Observing Self.** Boston Press, Massachusetts. First digital-print edition 2002.

Edinger, F.E. (1972), **Ego and Archetype.** Originally pub. by N.Y. Putnam 1972, reprint 1991 by Shambhala Publications, Inc.

Freke, T. and Gandy, P. (2001), **Jesus and the Lost Goddess.** New York, Three Rivers Press.

Harkness, D. (2014), **The Book of Life.** Headline Publishing Group.

Hauck, D.W. (2004), **Sorcerer's Stone – A Beginner's Guide to Alchemy.** New York, Citadel Press Books.

Jung, C.G. (1921), **Psychological Types, C.W. Vol 6.** Published in English in 1971 by Routledge.

Jung, C.G. (1953), **Two Essays on Analytical Psychology, C.W. Vol. 7.** Published by Routledge & Kegan Paul Ltd.

Jung, C.G. (1960), **The Structure and Dynamics of the Psyche. C.W. Vol 8.** Routledge & Kegan Paul Ltd. 2nd Edition (2014) by Routledge.

Jung, C.G. (1959), **Aion. Researches into the Phenomenology of the Self. C.W. Vol 9 Part II,** 2nd Edition. Routledge & Kegan Paul Ltd.

Jung C.G. (1953), **Psychology and Alchemy. C.W. vol. 12.**
Routledge & Kegan Paul Ltd. 2nd Edition 1968, 2nd Printing 1970.

Jung C.G. (1954), **The Practice of Psychotherapy. C.W. vol. 16.**
Routledge & Kegan Paul Ltd. 2nd Edition 1966. This printing 1981.

Kirkpatrick, J. (2000), **All Together in one Place.** WaterBrook Press, Colorado.

Kostova, E. (2010), **The Swan Thieves.** Little Brown Book Group.

Monroe, R.A. (1972), **Journeys Out of the Body.** Souvenir Press Ltd.

Monroe, R.A. (1986), **Far Journeys.** Souvenir Press Ltd.

Monroe, R.A. (1994), **Ultimate Journey.** Mainstream Books Edition Doubleday.

Moorjani, A. (2012), **Dying to be me.** Hay House UK Ltd.

Newton, M.(1994), **Journey of Souls.** Republished (2002) Llewellyn Publications.

Newton, M. (2000), **Destiny of Souls.** Llewellyn Publications.

Raff, J. (2000), **Jung and the Alchemical Imagination.** Nicolas-Hays, Inc. Berwick, ME.

Rank, Otto. (1989), **Art and Artist.** W.W. Norton & Company Ltd.

Rossi. (1977), **The Cerebral Hemispheres in Analytical Psychology.** In Journal of Analytical Psychology No. 22.

Samuels, A. (1986) **A Critical Dictionary of Jungian Analysis.** Routledge & Kegan Paul.

Stevens, A. (1982) **Archetype – A Natural History of the Self.** Routledge & Kegan Paul. Reprinted (1990) by Routledge.

The Urantia Foundation, (1955), **The Urantia Book.** Urantia Foundation, Chicago.

Separate Biographical Outlines relating to Cycles One, Two and Three

Cycle One:

As an adolescent, one of the most difficult and painful things I did was to turn my back on my religious upbringing. I had to break away from a whole edifice of beliefs, repetitive rituals and celebrations that could not satisfy my growing need for real spiritual guidance. I needed a living experience of God, not just parables and nursery stories.

I had to trust, that in my search for truth I would not be condemned for needing answers and seeking them wherever I could. As a child I wanted to 'know reality' since what surrounded me felt hollow and superficial. At the same time, I had a strong sense of spiritual homesickness and it was this that motivated me to keep searching for a way to my spiritual home.

My journey began in my twenties and from then until now I have kept a record of my journey. How? By recording the poems that erupted into my conscious mind. The first instance of a break-through from my unconscious to my conscious mind occurred when I was seven, as I have recorded in the Introduction, but it was another fourteen years before it happened again and this was the beginning of my spiritual journey.

As has happened several times in my life, the eruption of a large quantity of poems was accompanied by a dramatic change in my life. Until my twenties I had studied all sciences with the hope of becoming a doctor. However, I had failed to study maths and women were not welcome into the medical profession sixty years ago. Instead, I worked in medical research as a technician in one of the most prestigious colleges in London.

Imagine my horror and disillusionment when I was required to genetically breed animals, kill them, take out their eyes and experiment on them. I had no-one to talk to about this and struggled hard to decide whether it was ethical to sacrifice animals in order to find answers to illnesses causing blindness in humans.

The department was closing down and I was transferred to another institute's research programme. I was still clinging on to the ideal of medical research benefitting humanity. This time I was required to endlessly repeat techniques and experiments without any possibility of engaging in the creative side of research. Bored and disillusioned, I quit science altogether.

I had always been artistic and I wanted to spend time painting. However, I needed to earn a living as I didn't want to sponge off my parents. I was employed at a pharmaceutical company as a secretary, but was subsequently transferred to work in the laboratory, when they learnt of my science background.

I stayed in this job for years because of the company's magnificent social club. For the first time ever in my life I had a rich social life, fun and lots of activities to engage in – a drama group, a tennis club, a licensed clubhouse, dances – and I made some good friends. One of them encouraged me to apply for art-college, which I did and thence began five years at art colleges.

It was there that the other side of my mind – the irrational and artistic side was nurtured. It was a difficult process to liberate myself from the straight-jacket of rational logical thinking that had filled my early life and education. It was also at art college in a liberal studies class, that I first came across the notion of the False Self versus the True Self. This scared me because I recognised that I had yet to discover my True Self.

Thus began my drive to 'know myself'. I undertook many trainings. The first was a two-year weekly experiential and theoretical training at the Institute for the Development of Human Potential, a magnificent introduction to many aspects of self-development and an exploration into the world of psychology including its various schools of thought.

After art college, I trained as a teacher and worked as a supply teacher in some of the worst socially deprived areas of London. I was unable to get a permanent post, as art was not a desirable subject at the time of severe educational cuts in 1976.

I lived in a shared house with other art students for about twelve years. Some of us attended meetings at Centre House, a New Age spiritual centre in London where we studied spiritual teachings and learned to meditate, a very rich period. Meditation has been a fairly constant feature in my life since then, except when I was travelling. I was having personal therapy and engaged in activities such as yoga and modern dance. I was exploring life.

However, I felt I needed to extract myself from all that was familiar and put myself into new and alien situations, in order to see how far I had been able to divest myself of my early conditioning.

Thus, when I was 37, I went on a world trip, starting off with an Encounter Overland journey to Katmandu, with 16 other people I didn't know, ostensibly to visit my two brothers who had emigrated to Australia when I was nineteen.

During that trip I gave myself permission to do whatever I wanted and not restrict myself to any limits I felt were down to my childhood conditioning. I explored my sexuality and drugs. I think my spiritual guides were keeping me safe as I almost over-dosed on Afghan Black, a powerful resin of some drug, whilst in Katmandu. My strategy of exploring life's possibilities was dangerous but affective.

I travelled on to Australia with a girlfriend I had met on the Overland adventure and we stayed with my brother in Melbourne before she left to travel to New Zealand. My other brother lived in Brisbane and I travelled there by Greyhound coaches. Meeting and staying with them after twenty years apart was quite strange, but healing.

I spent several months travelling around Australia by coach and even climbed Ayers Rock, though that is no longer possible.

You may wonder – did I not want marriage and children? No. Family life had never appealed to me and I was too focused on my spiritual journey.

How did I support myself financially? In my first job as a research technician, I had plenty of time to spare whilst experiments 'cooked'. I used that time to teach myself to touch-type, a skill that has supported me over the years doing temp secretarial work.

Without it, I could never have recorded my poems or written this book.

When I returned to England, I felt lonely. I wanted someone to share my life with. I met my life-long partner through a personal ad in a London free magazine. I have no doubt in my own mind this was a meeting planned long before we were born.

He wanted to travel and we needed to accumulate funds to do so. We saved hard and then two events occurred, almost simultaneously, that boosted our savings. He sold a flat he had purchased and was fortunate in that it had increased considerably in value during the relatively short period he had owned it.

The second event, was that the landlord who owned the property that I and my fellow art students had rented for many years, wanted us to vacate the property. He offered us a generous lump sum of money to move out. The timing was perfect, and as we were all in agreement, we accepted his offer.

My share of this incentive payment boosted my savings, so that my partner and I now had sufficient capital to travel. I was then forty years of age and he was fifty. We were looking for new ways to earn a living.

We were together 24 hours a day as we travelled overland through Europe and on into Asia, roughing it to stretch our finances. The honeymoon phase was replaced by the hard process of getting to know each other.

I say it was no accident that we met. It provided the perfect opportunity for us to recognise that the wounds we had both sustained from our relationships with our mothers, had left us with a problem. We both had difficulty trusting women.

On my side the roots of that issue is clarified in the introduction. The situation with my partner was different. He had been abandoned by his mother very early on. She had been unable to deal with his crying and had taken him back to the hospital. Although she did eventually return to pick him up, the damage had already been done. He learned to mistrust women, fearing rejection and abandonment. We stayed together for 35 years, and learned a lot.

When we returned to England in 1988 after ten months travelling, we set up a business importing high quality arts and crafts from Asia and selling them here. However, the severe recession of the following year meant it foundered. Less people had the money for luxury items and we spent a few years working to clear up the debts we had accumulated.

Cycle Two:

As with all the Cycles, this one was characterised by a major change in life direction.

When we returned from travelling in 1988, we lived in *Bonnie*, a second-hand motorhome we had purchased in Frankfurt. We lived on a farm where we set up a workshop in an industrial building. We had registered 'Asiacraft' in 1989, selling high quality 'Arts and Crafts' from Asia.

Terry travelled extensively as a salesman and I was designing soft furnishings for the UK market, loosely based on Kashmiri rug designs, and getting them made up in Kashmir. These were very popular. However, another major UK recession in 1991 hit us badly and we had to cut our losses by closing Asiacraft in 1992.

I moved to a bed-sit in London and worked as a Medical Secretary. I had set up Diana Secretarial Services, which meant I could cut out the fees for an agency and earn more to pay off our debts. Terry remained in *Bonnie*, using his carpentry skills to build furniture, plus also working as a technician in a local school for the same reason.

We had both benefitted from counselling and therapy and had started a two-year counsellor training in 1990 with a view to setting up a Counselling Service. In 1992 and with the help of the Enterprise Allowance I had set up Diana Counselling Services and worked at a local GP practice. By then I had moved closer to Terry and he also worked at the same GP practice.

Terry's mother died in 1991 and when his father became unable to cope alone, Terry moved in and became his carer. I moved in, in January 1993 when my own father died. Terry's father died later that same year.

Having completed our training and gained experience as counsellors, we set up our counselling service in 1994, which continued to operate for twenty years.

I undertook further trainings in Park's Inner Child Therapy and Group Work trainings at the Richmond Fellowship. Terry was teaching counselling at college as well as seeing private clients including alcohol dependent clients.

There was another death in my family. My eldest brother died in Australia in 1997 from a brain tumour.

There is one major event that I need to include here for it catalysed the emergence of my alter ego / my shadow, which I termed my Goddess –an aspect of the True Self within me and informs much of the poetry in Cycle Two.

In 1998 aged 52, I applied to university to do an MA in counselling and psychotherapy. By then I had been working professionally as a counsellor / psychotherapist for six years. Although a member of a professional body, I wanted to gain my professional accreditation and I was missing the verification of a minor element required for that. I felt I could obtain that verification together with the stimulus of working with like-minded people, plus work towards an MA.

The course stipulated that in the first year we would be focused on Person-Centred counselling – something I was extremely familiar with. However, I noticed that certain typical characteristics of this model of counselling were missing from the way the tutors were teaching it. I confronted these omissions as I felt that they were misrepresenting the model to the students, many of whom had no experience of counselling at all.

I was shocked and humiliated by the reaction of the tutors, who verbally attacked me publicly in the group, accusing me of trying to undermine their authority and thus acquire or steal some of their power for myself. From then on, I became marked as a 'trouble-maker', which made for an uncomfortable experience. I kept my cool at the time, but it had profound implications for my inner process

I left the course at the end of the first year as I had achieved the minor element, which was one of the reasons I had applied for the course. This meant I could now apply for professional accreditation with my professional body.

At least twice before in my life men had obstructed my progress career-wise. On one occasion a tutor had destroyed work I had created, accidentally so he said, which meant it could not be submitted for evaluation. On the second separate occasion an assessor had failed my ceramic sculptures on the grounds they were 'art' and not 'craft'. My tutors at the time were humiliated, for although they violently disagreed with the assessor's decision, there was nothing they could do as the assessor was from an independent body, The Craftsman Potter's Association.

My inner Goddess/My Shadow was outraged at this latest example of bullying. It appeared that when I challenged men's authority or appeared to question their actions, they attacked me in whatever way they could. For the first time, my inner Goddess exploded into my conscious awareness. I had at last made contact with an aspect of my True Self. This is clearly recorded in the poems of Cycle Two.

Cycle Three:

As with the other Cycles, a change of life direction was imminent. Having retired from counselling I now focused on writing.

A brief history of my writing:

I had written a fable in 1982 called The Dragon and the Toad and subsequently refined it. It was intended as a children's book and

is a very simplistic version of alchemy in which the two opposites –
The Dragon and the Toad – ultimately unite to create a very happy
chameleon. (This is where I get my writer's name from, Camilla
Leon.) I wanted someone to illustrate it.

Linda and Roger Garland illustrated the first version of '*The Lord
of the Rings*' and just happened to have a gallery near to our beloved
'Windwhistle' holiday venue in Cornwall. We visited them in 2014
and loved their work. On impulse I asked if they ever took
commissions to which they replied 'Yes'. Much to my astonishment
they agreed to have a look at my fable and make a decision –and so
it began.

Roger produced a magnificently coloured cover design for the
book whilst Linda produced some extraordinarily beautiful images
for the story. Unfortunately, Roger was diagnosed with MND and
they had to end our contract. A disastrous prognosis for Roger who
sadly died in 2017.

My other brother in Australia knew all about this and 'by
chance' (!!!) just happened to bump into Andrew Plant – an
illustrator of children's books. A fertile period of exchanged emails
ensued and by 2018 I had a magnificently illustrated copy of the
fable.

The same year I took it to the Winchester Writer's Festival. I had
booked four children's book agents hoping to get a publisher. I had
described it as a children's book. All four agents loved the book but
were adamant it was not a children's book – it was too long and the
ideas and language too complex. In addition, many publishers prefer

to use their own illustrators. Thus, this little gem of a book languishes on my shelf.

My partner Terry had suffered from chronic heart problems for years and his health deteriorated. I became his full-time carer and he died in 2020 on my birthday. I am convinced he waited so that he could share my birthday with me and then gently passed away in the evening lying on his bed. He just missed the pandemic, for which I am deeply grateful. Of course, I miss his physical presence but would not wish him back. The last few years of his life were a torment for him. His body was worn out. He is alive in my heart and always will be.

Maybe it was being faced with my own eventual mortality, that spurred me on to consider how I might use my poems to inspire others to undertake their own spiritual journey. Having accompanied me on the difficult bits of this narrative I have included poems for my readers which illustrate the joys and benefits of making the effort. The last poem from my Muse was in June 2021 and is printed on page 4 of this book. Although the Three Cycles are apparently completed, the spiritual journey never ends and it keeps on giving and giving.